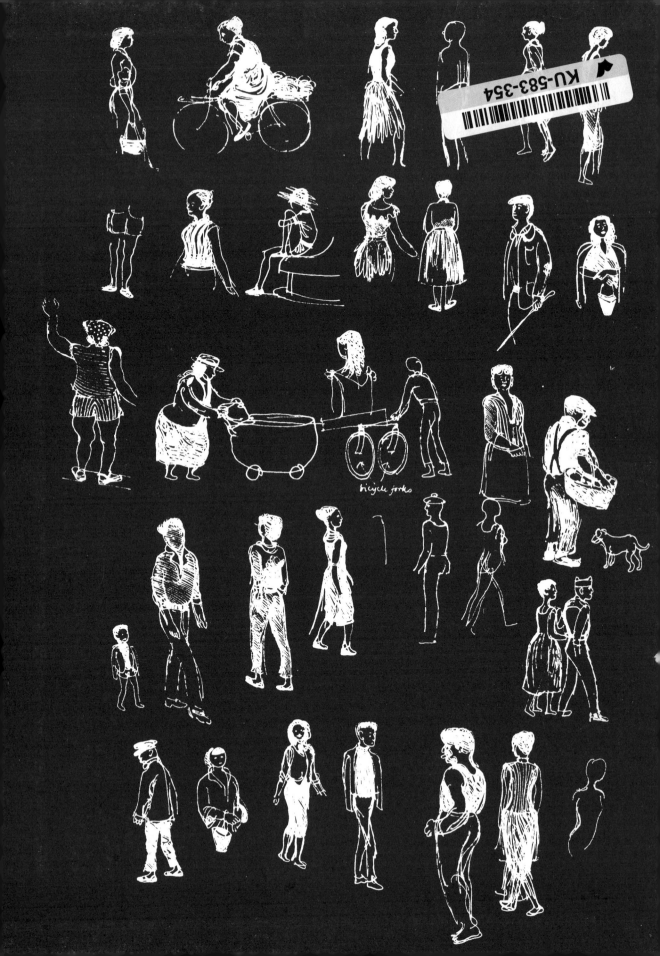

VOGUE

French Cookery

by Francine

drawings by David Gentleman

VOGUE

French Cookery

by Francine

edited by Mary Reynolds

drawings by David Gentleman

Collins — Glasgow & London
in association with
The Condé Nast Publications Ltd

William Collins Sons & Co Ltd
Glasgow London Sydney Auckland
Toronto Johannesburg

© The Condé Nast Publications Ltd
First published 1976
ISBN 0 00 435054 5

Made and printed in Great Britain by
William Collins Sons & Co Ltd Glasgow

Contents

Introduction

One of the consolations for my advanced age is the fact that my memory stretches back to the heyday of the *haute cuisine bourgeoise*, when every French hostess set a table that was almost the equal of their fine restaurants' of the time, and far superior to anything I knew in England. Moreover, many of these ladies not only employed expert *cuisinières*, but were able themselves to inspire, direct and, if necessary, deputize for them.

One such was Francine – Madame Cosette Vogel. (The g was soft, and the accent on the second syllable of the surname)

It must be acknowledged that it has never been easy for the foreigner to gain entry into French homes; but I enjoyed that privilege *chez les Vogel*, and was the more impressed by their gastronomic standards because I knew Francine, besides being the mother of three then young children, led a busy journalistic life which kept her long hours from their Paris *appartement* and only permitted brief week-ends at *La Faisanderie*. This was the ancient gamekeeper's house in the forest of St-Germain, to which they had harmoniously added a modern wing – the first place, incidentally, where I saw a circular, open fireplace, in the middle of a room, which did not smoke.

Francine came of an artistic and intellectual family. (Who was the chef who said he seasoned his sauces with brains?) One brother was the editor of *Vogue*, another the author/illustrator of the enchanting *Babar* books for children. She married Lucien Vogel, editor/publisher of the successful *Jardin des Modes*. Before then he had produced the elegant *Gazette du Bon Ton*, inspiration of the drawn covers of *Vogue* that have recently become so popular again. Later he invented *Vu*, the prototype of picture-news magazines such as *Picture Post* in England and *Life* in America. One of her daughters, having survived the concentration camps, became a prominent member of the *Chambre des Députés* – for better or worse, in the Communist Party.

Francine was a large (not fat) lady; no beauty, but with an engaging frankness of feature. She was forthright in the expression of her opinions; but in her family's voluble circle you had to be forthright, to be able to express any opinion at all.

Meals with the Vogels reminded me of the accounts in Colette's autobiographies of her mother's cooking – though Francine was not Burgundian by origin but, rather remotely, Alsatian. However, the Vogel table was not regional; it was eclectic, inspired by the best traditions of all French departments.

Though many of her recipes were rich, there was a fundamental simplicity in her personal *cuisine*. She preferred homely dishes, whose excellence came from the use of fresh material of prime quality, prepared with patient care. She had a respect for offal, and an economical appreciation of the cheaper cuts of meat which, by painstaking handling – one might almost say, by reverent handling – could be elevated to gourmet standards.

One must remember that there was no deep-freeze then, so all the ingredients were seasonal; but with all of France's culinary resources to draw on, that imposed no galling limitations to the menus. There were no electric blenders; but Francine's *pâtés* and *terrines* seem to me, in recollection, to have had a more satisfactory substance than the machine-made equivalents of today. Even refrigerators were then capricious in their functioning; fine judgement and studied experience were necessary for the ideal presentation of food. Francine did not eschew labour-saving devices, but she abhorred short cuts that scamped perfection.

The proof of her puddings, and other recipes, came in her servantless days in Manhattan during the Second War. Her husband's left-wing opinions had compelled escape before the Nazis. I had myself to spend a month in New York at the beginning of 1943, and I remember ploughing my way on foot one evening through a blizzard – no taxis could run, or none at any rate would – to their apartment on the East River. The weather is not irrelevant; it meant that Francine could not have nipped out to get something special for me. Yet with strange materials and but-recently acquired equipment, she served us, unaided, a truly memorable meal.

I remember her telling me how difficult it had been to get used to the new tools of her trade. (The conversation comes back – we were talking French, as mine was a little better than her English – because of an unfortunate confusion I made between *cocotte* and *cocotée*, which she had insisted must be heavy-bottomed.) She admired, with some reservations, the American provender; she was amused by their gadgets; but you needed, she said, your familiar *batterie de cuisine*. This need not be elaborate, and certainly not expensive; but adequate, *and right*, for its various jobs. I commend Chapter Two to the reader's attention.

Another of Francine's qualities was a fine nose for culinary talent. She would have made a good scout for the Michelin inspectors. You had only to hear of a new restaurant in Paris or the Ile de France, rush there to enjoy the first-fruits – and find Francine already installed, deep in conference with the fledgling *maître*, extracting new ideas for copy for her readers. For which, to do her justice, she offered reciprocal suggestions.

Cooking like hers requires intelligence, but not intellectualism; many of the best cooks are quite simple – but shrewd. It requires practice – which should console beginners whose first attempts are disappointing (and dare I add, at the risk of discouraging sales, even their second ones?). Above all, it requires patience. This is not the *cuisine* for the housewife-in-a-hurry. But if time is available, how can it be better spent, how used to give greater pleasure to others?

Fortunately, it seems to me, despite the contemporary rush of life, there are more and more young British hostesses prepared to give time to this exacting but delightful art. And who have the necessary intelligence. The following pages contain much inspiration for them.

H. W. Yoxall

Les Vins

French Wines for the Table and Kitchen

French wine is the natural partner of French food, and Francine suggested specific wines to serve with nearly all her recipes. But as many of the wines are now either difficult to find or prohibitive in price, the following notes are intended as a very general guide to choosing wine for the table and for the kitchen.

Choosing Table Wines to Partner Food

There are no absolutely hard and fast rules, and choice is really a matter of personal preference and availability. Basically, wine should either blend with and enhance the harmony of flavours in a good recipe, or it should emphasize them by contrast. For instance, a dry flavoured wine can be delicious with a rich and creamily sauced dish. But if a really fine wine is to be a feature of the meal then the food should be simple, of excellent quality, and plainly cooked so that it does not detract from the wine. Generally speaking, try to suit the 'weight' of the wine to the food. Strong flavoured foods like game or robust cheese need hearty wines with bold rather than subtle flavours, while delicate dishes are happiest with lighter wines.

If only one wine is being served, choose it to partner the main dish, and it can then be finished with the cheese which in France is always served immediately after the main course for this very reason.

When more than one wine is served, the generally accepted order of batting is a young wine before an older, a dry wine before a sweeter, and white before red except when the white is a sweet wine which would usually be served with the dessert.

Many wines today are sold under brand names, and the description on the label gives a fair idea of the contents of the bottle in terms of light, dry, semi-sweet, full and so on. In the case of French *Appellation Contrôlée* wines which are labelled only with their district names, or in the case of fine wines their vineyard name, the following notes give a general idea of their characteristics—although these, as everyone knows, tend to vary from year to year and from shipper to shipper.

White Wines

Loire wines such as Muscadet, Pouilly-Fumé or Sancerre: light Burgundies such as Chablis or Pouilly-Fuissé; or a Sylvaner or Zwicker from Alsace.   **Dry, light-bodied**

Serve with oysters, cold shellfish, plain grilled fish, egg dishes.

Mâcon Blanc; Riesling or Traminer from Alsace; Bordeaux from the Grâves district; or Burgundies such as Meursault or Puligny-Montrachet.   **Dry, full-bodied**

Serve with fish, poultry or veal dishes with creamy sauces.

Sauternes, Barsac, etc.   **Sweet**

Serve with puddings, ices and desserts.

Red Wines

Mâcon Rouge; Beaujolais, Fleurie, Juliénas, Côtes-du-Rhône, or light Bordeaux wines such as Médoc, St. Julien or Margaux.   **Dry, medium-bodied**

Serve with roast chicken, turkey, veal, lamb or beef, liver, foie gras, soft paste cheeses like Brie, cheese dishes.

Fuller Bordeaux wines such as St Emilion or Pomerol; Beaune; all the great Burgundies such as Corton, Pommard, Volnay, Chambertin, or the big Rhône wines such as Châteauneuf-du-Pape or Hermitage.   **Dry, full-bodied**

Serve with game, meat marinated in red wine, duck and goose, kidneys and strong flavoured cheeses.

Rosé Wines

These come from various districts, and range from dryish (Tavel) to medium-sweet (Anjou Cabernet).

Serve with any light dishes with non-assertive flavours, and especially with cold meats and picnic food.

Sparkling Wines

Some people enjoy dry or medium sparkling wines right through a meal, others as an apéritif only. The sweet types are best reserved for desserts and gâteaux. The descriptions of the sweetness or otherwise of champagne and other sparkling wines can be misleading. The generally accepted classifications are as follows:

Champagne		Sparkling Wines	
Brut	— dry	Brut	— dry
Nature	— dry	Sec	— dry
Sec	— medium	Demi-Sec	— medium
Demi-Sec	— sweet	Moelleux	— sweet
Doux	— sweet	Doux	— sweet

Serving Temperatures

White, rosé and sparkling wines are at their best when lightly chilled to emphasize their refreshing qualities. Half an hour to an hour in the main body of the refrigerator should be sufficient, or serve them in an ice bucket.

Red wines should, if possible, be allowed to stand in the dining room for several hours to reach room temperature. Then, if the cork is removed an hour before serving the wine will have the best chance to develop its full quality.

Other Wines and Spirits for Cooking

Exceedingly useful in dishes calling for a combination of white wine and herbs. It is roughly twice the strength of a table wine so you need less of it. **Dry white vermouth**

Adds a wonderful richness to sauces for chicken, ham or consommés. Although the result is different, try medium-dry sherry if Madeira is not available. **Dry Madeira**

Often used in sweet dishes. Their flavours are highly concentrated, so a tablespoon or two will suffice, and too much can spoil the effect. An orange based liqueur such as Grand Marnier, Cointreau or Curaçao is the most frequently used. Kirsch adds distinction to creamy mixtures and ices, and fruit brandies to fruits and ices. **Liqueurs**

Not a native product but often used either to flavour or flame desserts. The type used in France is usually a dark Jamaican rum. **Rum**

The spirit of the French kitchen for both savoury and sweet dishes. Naturally one does not use a fine liqueur brandy but it must be a sound one. **Brandy**

Cooking with Wine

Wine is much more than just a flavouring ingredient, it enriches and adds a fillip to the simplest dish, and is a wonderfully effective tenderizer for the tougher cuts of meat.

The amount needed varies from a few tablespoons to half a pint or so. Small amounts can sometimes be taken from the wine you are serving with the meal. But if you are buying wine specifically for the kitchen, choose a young, dryish wine with good flavour and body—a white wine of the type listed under 'Dry, full-bodied' (page 11) for instance, or a red wine of the 'Dry, medium-bodied' type (page 11). While one obviously does not buy a vintage wine to cook with, it is important not to use a thin or acid wine which will do nothing to improve a dish and may even spoil it.

The important point to remember about using wine in recipes is that it must be *cooked* sufficiently to evaporate the alcohol leaving only its flavour and 'body' to enrich the dish. This happens automatically in slowly simmered casseroles and long cooking dishes. When making 'quick' sauces, you achieve similar results by boiling the wine furiously for a few minutes to drive off the alcohol and to concentrate and mellow the flavour.

About Flaming

The object of flaming is to refine a dish by burning up excess fat, at the same time leaving behind the 'essence' of the spirit to enhance the flavour. Although other spirits can be used, brandy is ideal because it combines a high proof spirit with a concentrated flavour. Orange based liqueurs are often used for flaming sweet dishes.

To ensure immediate ignition warm the spirit in a soup ladle or tiny saucepan then light it and pour it flaming over the food. For safety's sake avert your face, and take care because the flames can be very lively, especially if the dish contains excess fat or sugar. Shake the pan gently to distribute the flames and bring the spirit into contact with as much of the food as possible. Wait until the flames die before adding other ingredients.

Batterie de Cuisine

Kitchen Equipment

In addition to the normal range of pots and pans found in most kitchens the following items of French kitchen equipment would be especially useful when making the recipes in this book. They are not essential but each was designed for its particular function.

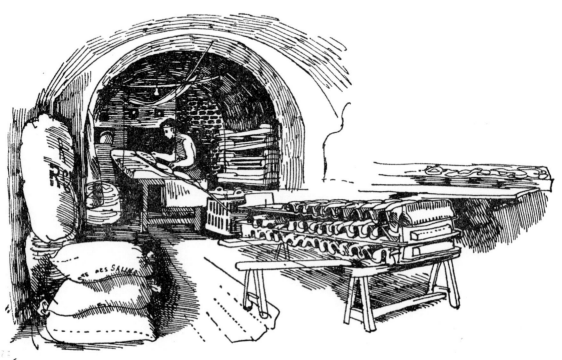

A selection in various sizes, round and oval, all with tight fitting lids, for all the slow cooking dishes. One at least should be a really large 4–6 litre (7–10 pint) capacity for braising large cuts of meat, a tongue or a chicken—the all purpose utensil known in France as a Fait-Tout or Daubière. Especially useful and versatile are the enamelled cast iron or cast aluminium casseroles which can be used on top of the cooker as well as in the oven. Their heavy ground bases make them suitable for electric, solid fuel or gas cookers.

Certain French earthenware cocottes can also be used over direct heat provided they are handled with care, and preferably used in conjunction with an asbestos or wire mat.

Cocottes
Casseroles

Useful if stock in large quantities is being made frequently, because the tall shape ensures the minimum of evaporation. Small amounts can be made in a large saucepan.

Marmite
Stock-pot or Stew-pot

This is an invaluable aid for spreading direct flames under earthenware or thin metal pans and helping to prevent catching and burning.

Brise-Flamme
Asbestos or Wire Mat

A pointed fine mesh sieve for straining sauces.

Chinois
Conical Sieve

A heavy, thick wooden board without joins on which to cut up meat and vegetables, and for chopping small amounts of herbs, etc. These jobs cannot be done on laminated plastic surfaces without blunting the knives.

Planche à Hâcher
Chopping Board

A selection of sharp knives is indispensable. Essential are a small paring knife for fruit and vegetables, a saw-edged stainless knife for slicing fruit, and traditional French cooks' knives in several sizes for cutting and chopping.

Couteaux de Cuisine
Cooks' Knives

Freshly ground peppercorns are an essential ingredient in practically all French savoury recipes.

Moulin à Poivre
Pepper Mill

In spite of modern electric blenders, there are still some jobs which need a really hard pounding in an old-fashioned mortar.

Mortier
Pestle and Mortar

These shallow flameproof dishes are essential for recipes in which a wide surface area for fast browning is needed.

Plats à Gratin
Gratin Dishes

For sweet pastry flans, fluted metal rings with removable bases give the best results. Plain rings can be used on ordinary flat baking trays. It is useful to have several sizes.

Tourtières
Flan Tins

These oval or round earthenware or china dishes with lids are decorative for baking, and serving unmoulded pâtés.

Terrines
Pâté Dishes

However, they are by no means essential as pâtés can be cooked in soufflé or pie dishes, or in casseroles.

Timbales à Soufflé
Soufflé Dishes

Straight-sided, flameproof, porcelain dishes are ideal for making and serving soufflés.

Ramequins
Ramekins

These are individual size soufflé dishes ideal for baking eggs, custards and mousses, and for serving individual portions.

Poêle à Omelette
Omelet Pan

For a single portion two egg omelet, you need a 15–18 cm (6–7 inch) pan with a flat base and sloping sides. Larger omelets can be cooked in heavy based non-stick frying pans.

Poêle à Crêpes
Pancake Pan

This is a small, very shallow iron pan, designed to facilitate the quick cooking and tossing of pancakes. But a small frying or omelet pan 15–18 cm (6–7 inches) in diameter is perfectly adequate.

Sautoir
Sauté Pan

This kind of wide, shallow saucepan with lid is invaluable for dishes requiring a quick initial frying followed by a short period of simmering. The handle enables the cook to shake the pan frequently. The base of the pan needs to be heavy, and a good conductor of heat, to ensure even cooking.

Soupière
Soup Tureen

No French kitchen would be without a family size earthenware or porcelain tureen in which the soup is served.

Mouli-Légumes
Vegetable Mill

This inexpensive hand operated sieve comes with two sizes of mesh and is indispensable for puréeing soups. Electric blenders are not suitable for soups containing tough skins, seeds or rinds.

Fouets
Wire Whisks

These open wire whisks are much used by chefs and quickly adopted by anyone who has worked with chefs. A small fouet is ideal for making smooth sauces and a large one for beating egg whites.

Mandoline
Universal Slicer

This is a flat slicer and shredder with adjustable blades. Ideal for slicing potatoes and other vegetables evenly and rapidly.

Les Provisions de la Cuisine Française

Ingredients for French Cooking

On the face of it, one might reasonably assume that most ingredients are the same the world over. But in the case of French raw materials there are subtle differences in flavours and textures, or in the way they are used, which result in a dish having a character which is definitely 'French' as distinct from 'English'. Cheese is a case in point – a gratin dish prepared with grated Gruyère and Parmesan has an altogether different character from one made with grated Cheddar. Self-raising flour is unknown in France, and French sausagemeat consists of nothing but well seasoned pure minced pork. The use of malt vinegar instead of wine vinegar spells ruin to the flavour of any dressing purporting to be French.

So, if you want to give your dishes authenticity the following notes on basic ingredients will help you choose the ones that most resemble their French originals.

Bacon

The kind of bacon usually used in French recipes is unsalted and unsmoked. The nearest British equivalent is pickled or salt belly pork, or unsmoked streaky bacon.

Barding Fat

Used for pâtés, tying over the breasts of poultry before roasting, etc. This is a *thin* slice of fresh pork fat preferably from the back just beneath the skin. If not available use thin rashers of unsmoked, fat, streaky bacon.

Bread Crumbs

Brown crumbs are required for sprinkling over the surface of dishes to be gratinéed or for coating food before frying. They are made by drying pieces of white bread in a slow oven until golden, and then crushing to fine crumbs with a rolling pin. *White crumbs* are made in the same way but they are not allowed to brown. Mixed with cheese they make a very crisp surface when gratinéed.

Butter

Unsalted and made from matured cream, French butter has an especially creamy flavour. If not available use a very mildly salted butter. Mixing butter with oil for frying reduces the temperature at which the butter begins to turn brown. To clarify butter for frying, simply melt over moderate heat, allow to settle for a few minutes, and then pour gently through muslin leaving the sediment behind in the pan.

Cheese

The cheeses commonly used in French cooking are Parmesan, Gruyère or Emmentaler, or a mixture of these. While these varieties give an especially fine and authentic flavour, it is, of course, possible to use other hard grating cheeses of good flavour. Petit suisse is a widely distributed French cream cheese.

Coffee

French preference is for strong black coffee made by a filter method from dark roast coffee beans.

Cream

French *crème fraîche* is thick and has roughly the same butter fat content as British double cream, but with a more 'matured' flavour.

Croûtes

Crisp, dried bread slices to serve with soups, etc. To make them, cut $\frac{1}{2}$-cm ($\frac{1}{4}$-inch) thick slanting slices from a French *baton* loaf. Bake in a slow oven for about 30 minutes until pale brown and crisp. For garlic croûtes rub the bread with a cut clove of garlic and sprinkle with olive oil before baking.

Croûtons

Cut $\frac{1}{2}$-cm ($\frac{1}{4}$-inch) thick slices of firm bread into $\frac{1}{2}$-cm ($\frac{1}{4}$-inch) cubes. Fry slowly in hot shallow oil and butter until evenly crisp and golden. Drain thoroughly and serve hot.

Flour	British plain, white, household flour has roughly the same composition as French flour and will give similar results in most home baking.
Garlic	A clove of garlic is one segment taken from a bulb of garlic. Well wrapped in kitchen foil, a bulb of garlic will keep well in the refrigerator. To crush garlic, peel it, sprinkle it liberally with salt and mash it to a paste on the corner of a chopping board, using a knife, or use a pestle and mortar.
Herbs	The herbs most used in France are parsley, chives, thyme, tarragon, chervil and bay. In the South, fennel, basil, sage and oregano join the list. Fresh herbs are naturally best, but some of the dried herbs retain their aromatic qualities well, especially those imported from Provence. Dried fennel stalks are imported or can be prepared from home-grown fennel.

Bouquet Garni This classic 'bouquet' of flavouring herbs consists of 2 to 3 stalks of fresh parsley, a sprig of thyme and a bay leaf, all tied together to facilitate removal before the dish is served. Additions to the basic bouquet include a piece of celery, a spring of fennel or marjoram, or a strip of dried orange peel. When dried herbs are used they are tied in a piece of muslin.

Fines Herbes A classic mixture of roughly equal quantities of chopped fresh parsley, chives, chervil and, when available, tarragon.

Jus de Viande This is the jellied meat essence which collects beneath the solidified fat when meat dripping is poured off from the roasting tin. It is a most valuable flavouring ingredient for brown sauces or special gravies.

Mustard The made-up mustard sold in attractive jars in France consists of mustard flour mixed with grape juice or wine vinegar and flavoured with herbs and spices. For use in sauces, choose a good yellow coloured mustard which will not harm the appearance of the sauce.

Oil Good olive oil is an essential ingredient in Mediterranean cooking, but in other parts of France ground nut or other pure vegetable oils are preferred.

Pepper Unless the recipe states otherwise, use good quality black peppercorns in a pepper mill and grind them freshly as required.

Pork Rind Thinly cut fresh pork rind is used to add a rich gelatinous quality to casserole dishes and stews.

Pork Sausage Meat	In France this contains no starch filler and is simply pure pork and pork fat minced, and seasoned with salt, pepper and spices. The best substitute is fresh, fairly fat pork, minced and well seasoned.
Salt	For preference use block salt or rock salt crystals.
Shallots	These small members of the onion family are easier to grow than they are to buy. Their virtue is that they soften rapidly when chopped and fried and have an attractive onion flavour. If not available use a mild onion.
Sugar	French household sugar is similar to British caster sugar.
Truffles	These pungent, and now rare, black fungi are available in cans at a huge price. Although Francine used truffles extensively, their use in recipes today must be optional, and in any case much of their original quality is lost in canning.
Vanilla Sugar	Vanilla-flavoured caster sugar is very easily made by keeping a couple of vanilla pods in the storage jar with the sugar. Remember to refill the jar when some of the sugar is used.
Vinegar	Red or white wine vinegars are used in French recipes, never malt vinegar. Herb flavoured vinegars are easily prepared by steeping sprays of fresh herbs in the bottle of wine vinegar. Tarragon vinegar is especially useful for salad dressings and Béarnaise Sauce.

Fonds de Cuisine

Basic Preparations

Many of the foundation preparations which give French cooking its special savour, such as stocks and marinades, are very simple to prepare. For convenience they have been grouped together in this chapter.

Stocks

The quality of many soups, sauces and casserole dishes depends to a large extent on a good stock base. Far from being extravagant, stocks are a means of extracting the utmost flavour from bones, trimmings and carcases which would otherwise be wasted. Small amounts can be made whenever the ingredients are available (poultry or game carcases for instance), and any surplus stock can be frozen and stored for up to 3 months. Bulk purchases of beef or veal for the freezer often provide a useful supply of raw bones. A well-flavoured stock is a natural by-product when boiling a chicken or a piece of beef. Stock cubes are invaluable for strengthening a weak stock, and can, when necessary, provide the stock itself.

Fonds de Volaille
Chicken Stock

Break up the carcase and put into a heavy saucepan with the giblets. Roughly cut up the carrot, celery, onion (washed not peeled) and tomato, and add to the pan with all the remaining ingredients. Add just enough water to cover. Bring to the boil and simmer, covered, for 1¼ hours, or pressure cook for 20 minutes. Strain, reduce if necessary to concentrate the flavour, and cool. Makes about 500 ml (1 pint) of stock.

A carcase of a cooked chicken
the giblets (excluding the liver), washed
1 large carrot, peeled
1 stick celery, washed
1 medium onion, washed but not peeled
1 ripe tomato (optional)
1 bay leaf
1 teaspoon salt
6 peppercorns
6 tablespoons dry white wine *or* vermouth (optional)

Fonds Brun
Bone Stock

Ask the butcher to chop the bones into small pieces. Put into a large, heavy saucepan and cover with cold water. Bring slowly to simmering point and simmer for 5 minutes, removing the scum as it accumulates on the surface. Chop the vegetables roughly and add to the pan with all the other ingredients. Bring back to the boil, skim, then simmer very gently, with the lid tilted, for 4–5 hours, or pressure cook for 40 minutes. Strain into a basin, and when cold remove the solidified fat from the surface.

1 kg (2 lb) beef or veal bones
1 large carrot, scraped
1 large onion, peeled
1 large stick celery, washed
1 bay leaf
3 sprigs parsley
2 cloves
3 peppercorns
1 teaspoon salt

La Gelée
Jellied Meat Stock

This rich jellied stock is used in a number of Francine's sauces, casseroles and meat dishes. Although 250 ml (½-pint) is usually the amount needed to add body and flavour to a recipe for four people, any surplus can be frozen.

Ask the butcher to roughly chop the knuckle of veal and to dice the shin of beef. Put into a heavy saucepan with the sliced onion and carrot, and all the other ingredients. Set over the lowest possible heat, cover, and cook until the juices are running and beginning to caramelize. Add 1½ litres (2½ pints) water and bring slowly to simmering point, removing the scum as it rises. Cover the pan and simmer very gently for about 3 hours. Strain the liquid into a bowl, and when cold remove the fat which has solidified on top of the jellied stock. Use as required.

450 g (1 lb) knuckle of veal
450 g (1 lb) shin of beef
1 onion, peeled
1 carrot, peeled
1 Bouquet Garni (p. 22)
1 raw chicken carcase, if available
6 black peppercorns, crushed
2 level teaspoons salt

Fumet de Poisson
Concentrated Fish Stock

1 kg (2 lb) white fish heads, bones
  and skin
2 onions, peeled
several sprigs parsley
1 small sprig thyme
1 small bay leaf
½ tablespoon lemon juice
125 ml (¼ pint) dry white wine
2 level teaspoons salt
6 black peppercorns

Cut the fish into pieces. Chop the onions and put into a large saucepan with the fish and all the other ingredients. Cover with 750 ml (1½ pints) cold water and bring slowly to the boil. Skim. Simmer with the lid tilted for 1 hour. Line a strainer with muslin and strain the stock, which should have reduced to about 500 ml (1 pint). Use as directed in the recipe.

Court Bouillon
Stock for Poaching Fish

1 carrot, peeled
1 leek, washed
1 onion, peeled
3 tablespoons white wine
3 tablespoons white wine vinegar
Bouquet Garni (p. 22)
1½ level tablespoons salt
8 black peppercorns

In France fish is never poached in water but in a flavoured stock. Slice the carrot, leek and onion. Put into a large saucepan or fish kettle with 1 litre (scant 2 pints) cold water and all the other ingredients. Bring slowly to the boil then cover and simmer for 30 minutes. Use hot or cold according to the recipe.

Mirepoix
Vegetable Base

100 g (4 oz) lean raw bacon or ham
  scraps
100 g (4 oz) carrots, scraped
2 sticks celery, washed
1 medium onion, peeled
25 g (1 oz) butter
½ bay leaf
1 sprig thyme
salt and ground black pepper

A mirepoix forms the base of many sauces and is also used as a bed on which to braise joints, hearts or poultry.

Chop the bacon or ham, and coarsely chop the vegetables. Melt the butter in a heavy based pan, add the vegetables and fry until golden, stirring frequently. Add the herbs and seasoning. Use as directed in the recipe.

Marinade

2 or 3 small onions, peeled
1 clove garlic, peeled
1 carrot, scraped
500 ml (1 pint) robust red wine
1 tablespoon brandy
4 tablespoons wine vinegar
1 Bouquet Garni (p. 22)
1 bay leaf
1 clove
2 level teaspoons salt
6 black peppercorns

To marinate meat, game or poultry is to steep it in a mixture of wine, herbs and vegetables for a few hours, or sometimes for a few days. The purpose is to tenderize tough cuts of meat and to add flavour. A little oil is added if the meat is especially dry.

Slice the onions, garlic and carrot and put it into a deep china or earthenware container with all the other ingredients. Use as directed in the recipe.

For a *Rich Marinade*, replace the vinegar with brandy.

Pâte à Crêpes
Basic Pancake Batter

Sift the flour and salt into a mixing bowl. Beat in the eggs and oil, and then, little by little, beat in about three-quarters of the milk, making a smooth batter. Set aside in a cool place for at least 1 hour before using, and then, if the mixture has become too thick, add more milk (or water) a little at a time.

200 g (8 oz) plain flour
pinch salt
3 eggs
1 tablespoon oil
about 500 ml (1 pint) milk

This quantity will make about 16 pancakes in an 18–20 cm (7–8 inch) frying pan.

To make pancakes Have a small pan containing about 2 tablespoons of oil *or* melted lard beside the cooker. Pour a little fat into the pancake pan, swirl it around then tip the surplus back into the saucepan leaving the pan just filmed with fat. Heat the frying pan until *very* hot, pour in enough batter just to cover the base *thinly*, and cook briskly for about 1 minute until set. Turn, or toss and cook the other side for about half a minute. Turn out flat, either on to a piece of greaseproof paper if they are to be filled and rolled immediately, or stack them one on top of another on an ovenproof dish, cover, and keep warm. Pancakes can also be made several hours in advance and reheated when needed; suitably wrapped they will keep for 2–3 days in the refrigerator, or for up to 1 month in a home freezer.

Pâte à Frire
Frying Batter

100 g (4 oz) plain flour
pinch salt
2 tablespoons oil
125 ml (¼ pint) tepid water *or* light
    ale
1 egg white

Sift the flour and salt into a basin. Stir in the oil and then the water or ale, mixing to a smooth cream. Leave to stand for at least 1 hour. Shortly before using, whisk the egg white stiffly and fold into the batter.

Pâte Brisée
Rich Shortcrust Pastry

150 g (6 oz) plain flour
large pinch salt
1 level teaspoon caster sugar
100 g (4 oz) firm butter
1–2 tablespoons cold water to mix

Sift the flour, salt and sugar into a mixing bowl. Cut the butter into 1 cm (⅓-inch) pieces and rub lightly into the flour with your fingers until the mixture resembles oat flakes. Don't over mix as further blending takes place later. Sprinkle in enough water to bind the mixture into a firm but pliable dough. Place on a lightly floured surface. Using the heel of the right hand press the pastry a little at a time down the board making a 'smear' 15–20 cm (6–8 inches) long. Gather the pastry into a ball and repeat once more. This process is known as the *fraisage*. Cover the pastry, or wrap in foil, and refrigerate for at least 2 hours.

This amount of pastry will line a 20 cm (8 inch) flan ring. It will keep for 3–4 days in the refrigerator or 1 month in a home freezer.

Les Sauces
et les Beurres Composés
Sauces and Flavoured Butters

Sauces, they say, can make or mar the reputation of a cook. But what is much more relevant for most of us today is the fact that an interesting sauce can transform otherwise everyday food into something rather special. With the help of a distinguished French sauce simple fare such as eggs, white fish, or a fresh vegetable can take their place as a separate course.

French household sauces are not extravagant and are much easier to make than many people suppose. The essential elements are good quality fresh ingredients, and a little care and attention over the details of temperature, timing, consistency and seasoning.

To keep sauces hot stand the saucepan containing the sauce in a larger pan, or a deep baking tin, containing hot water. In the case of flour-thickened or purée sauces, the surrounding water can be allowed to simmer, but for delicate melted butter sauces such as Hollandaise, Béarnaise or Beurre Blanc it should be no more than tepid. This is the method known as *au bain marie*.

To prevent a skin forming on flour-thickened sauces keep them tightly covered with a lid while in the *bain marie*. If the sauce is to be cooled and reheated later, then film the surface with water which can later be beaten into the sauce.

Sauce Béarnaise
Béarnaise Sauce

Leave the butter in a warm atmosphere so that it softens but does not melt. Put the vinegar, peppercorns and shallot into a small saucepan and simmer until just 1 tablespoon of liquid remains. Strain through a *fine* sieve into a small basin. Rest the basin over a saucepan of warm water so that the basin does not touch the water. Set over *low* heat and take care not to allow it to boil. Add the cold water and about 15 g ($\frac{1}{2}$-oz) of the butter to the vinegar reduction. Add the beaten egg yolks and beat with a small wire whisk until the egg thickens. *Immediately* begin beating in the softened butter, about 15 g ($\frac{1}{2}$-oz) at a time. When all is amalgamated and the sauce thick and creamy, stir in the herbs, and adjust the seasoning if necessary.

Serve this superb sauce *warm* (but not hot) with beef steaks, noisette of lamb, fish, chicken or egg dishes.

Note: Overheating at any time will cause separation and curdling.

100 g (3–4 oz) unsalted butter
4 tablespoons tarragon vinegar
4 peppercorns, crushed
1 teaspoon chopped shallot
1 tablespoon cold water
2 egg yolks, beaten
1 teaspoon finely chopped fresh tarragon
1 teaspoon finely chopped fresh parsley

Sauce Béchamel
Basic White Sauce

This sauce, based on a white roux (butter and flour cooked together), is one that Francine used frequently, in varying degrees of thickness. The method given, of whisking the *hot* liquid into the roux with a small wire whisk, produces a smooth, lump-free sauce very quickly. It is important to the flavour to cook the roux gently for 2–3 minutes before adding the liquid, and to simmer it for at least 5 minutes after adding the liquid. When using a wire whisk you cannot, of course, use a non-stick pan.

The thickness of the sauce depends on the proportion of flour to liquid as follows:

	thin pouring sauce	medium coating sauce	very thick soufflé base
butter	20 g ($\frac{3}{4}$ oz)	30 g ($1\frac{1}{4}$ oz)	45 g ($1\frac{3}{4}$ oz)
plain flour	15 g ($\frac{1}{2}$ oz)	25 g (1 oz)	40 g ($1\frac{1}{2}$ oz)
hot milk	250 ml ($\frac{1}{2}$ pint)	250 ml ($\frac{1}{2}$ pint)	250 ml ($\frac{1}{2}$ pint)
salt and pepper to taste			

Melt the butter in a heavy based saucepan, add the flour and cook, stirring, over *low* heat for 2 minutes. Don't allow the roux to brown. Off the heat pour in the hot liquid all at once and beat briskly with a wire whisk to blend thoroughly the liquid and roux. Return to a moderate heat and stir with the whisk until the sauce is boiling. Simmer for 5 minutes, stirring occasionally. Remove from the heat and season to taste.

Variations

Sauce Velouté Make a coating sauce using concentrated chicken, veal or fish stock instead of milk, and finish it with a little cream.

Sauce Crème Add 3–4 tablespoons double cream to a coating sauce and finish with a few drops of lemon juice.

Sauce Mornay To a coating sauce add 50 g (2 oz) of grated cheese (ideally mixed Parmesan and Gruyère), a shake of cayenne and a grating of nutmeg. Don't add additional butter or cream if the sauce is to be browned under the grill.

Sauce Mornay à la Crème Add 125 ml ($\frac{1}{4}$-pint) dry white wine to a coating Béchamel Sauce and simmer for 5–10 minutes while the sauce reduces a little. Off the heat whisk in one egg yolk mixed with a tablespoon of double cream, and 50 g (2 oz) of grated Parmesan and Gruyère cheese mixed. Heat gently but do not boil, and add seasoning to taste.

Sauce Aurore Stir in by degrees about 3 tablespoons of thick fresh Tomato Purée (p. 40). Check the seasoning.

Beurre Blanc
Shallot Butter

4 shallots, peeled
4 tablespoons white wine vinegar
salt and white pepper
150 g (6 oz) unsalted butter

Chop the shallots very finely, until almost a purée. Put into a small saucepan with the vinegar and seasonings, and cook over low heat until the shallots are tender and the vinegar reduced to $1\frac{1}{2}$ tablespoonfuls. Remove from the heat and leave in the pan to cool. Have the butter at room temperature and beat it to a cream. Just before serving, set the pan over a *very low* beat and whisk in the butter 15 g ($\frac{1}{2}$-oz) at a time. The butter must *not melt*, but emulsify with the shallots to form a creamy consistency. Check the seasoning, and serve right away in a barely warm bowl.

There are many ways of making this sauce—some cooks make it quite runny. Here it is the consistency of a mayonnaise.

An excellent sauce with freshwater fish or any plain boiled fish.

Beurres Composés
Flavoured Butters

Flavoured butters are a simple but effective way of adding a finishing touch to plain foods such as grilled meat or fish, and boiled vegetables. They can also be used for spreading canapés and for enriching soups. For garnishing purposes form the flavoured butter into a $1\frac{1}{2}$ cm ($\frac{3}{4}$-inch) diameter roll, and chill. Cut into rounds and use as required.

Beurre d'Escargots Cream 50 g (2 oz) unsalted butter with 1 tablespoon grated shallot, 1–2 crushed cloves garlic, 1 tablespoon finely chopped parsley, and salt and pepper to taste. This is the classic garlicky butter used for snails.

Beurre Maître d'Hôtel Cream 50 g (2 oz) unsalted butter with 2 teaspoons lemon juice, 1 tablespoon finely chopped parsley, and salt and pepper.

Beurre de Crevettes ou d'Écrevisses Wash the tail shells of a handful of shrimps, prawns or crayfish to remove excess salt. Dry them and pound thoroughly in a mortar. Work in an equal weight of unsalted butter, then heat very gently until melted. Pass through a fine sieve, add a few drops of carmine if wished, and leave to cool.

Sauce Bordelaise
Red Wine Sauce

Ask the butcher to saw the marrow bone into several pieces. Remove the marrow from the bone and poach it in gently simmering salted water for about 5 minutes. Drain and set aside. Put the wine, shallots, thyme and bay leaf into a saucepan and simmer, uncovered, until only one third of the liquid is left. Add the aspic or consommé and the butter. Pass through a fine nylon sieve and return to the saucepan. Blend the cornflour with a tablespoon of cold water, stir into the sauce and continue stirring until boiling. Chop the marrow into small dice, add to the sauce with the parsley. Check the seasoning and continue simmering gently for several minutes. Makes about 250 ml ($\frac{1}{2}$ pint) of sauce.

1 large marrow bone
salt
125 ml ($\frac{1}{4}$ pint) red wine
1 tablespoon chopped shallots
1 sprig thyme
half a bay leaf
175 m. ($\frac{1}{3}$ pint) aspic jelly *or* canned consommé
25 g (1 oz) butter
2 level teaspoons cornflour
ground black pepper
1 tablespoon chopped parsley

Sauce Dumas
Cold Tomato and Herb Sauce

Put the tomatoes and their juice into a heavy saucepan and simmer over low heat, uncovered, until most of the juice has evaporated. Mash the tomatoes with a wooden spoon, and continue simmering until reduced to a thick, rough purée. Set aside until cold. Stir the mustard into the tomatoes, then stir in the oil drop by drop, as for a mayonnaise. Add the shallots, herbs, vinegar and salt and pepper to taste. Makes about 250 ml ($\frac{1}{2}$-pint) of sauce.

This sauce is delicious with all kinds of fish, and goes well with plainly cooked eggs and chicken.

1 (800 g or 28 oz) can peeled tomatoes
1 level tablespoon made yellow mustard
3–4 tablespoons oil
1 teaspoon finely chopped shallot
2 teaspoons chopped mixed fresh herbs e.g. chervil, tarragon, parsley, chives
1–2 teaspoons wine vinegar
salt and ground black pepper

Sauce Espagnole
Basic Brown Sauce

1 medium onion, peeled
1 medium carrot, peeled
2 sticks celery, washed
100 g (4 oz) lean cooked bacon *or* ham
75 g (3 oz) beef *or* pork dripping *or* butter
50 g (2 oz) flour
750 ml (1½ pints) brown stock *or* canned consommé
1 level tablespoon tomato purée
1 large bay leaf
1 large sprig parsley
1 large sprig thyme
salt and ground black pepper
2 tablespoons medium dry Madeira *or* sherry

Chop the onion, carrot, celery and bacon or ham. Heat the fat in a heavy based saucepan and over *low* heat fry the onion, carrot, celery and ham, covered, for about 10 minutes. Stir in the flour, and cook very gently so that it slowly turns nut brown, stirring frequently. Add the stock or consommé, tomato purée, herbs and seasonings, and bring to the boil, whisking frequently with a wire whisk. Cover, and simmer gently for 1 hour or longer, occasionally skimming off any fat or scum that rises to the surface. Press the sauce through a fine sieve, and continue simmering until it will lightly coat the back of a spoon. If it reduces too much during cooking, add a little more stock. Finally, add the Madeira or sherry and check the seasoning.

This quantity makes about 500 ml (1 pint) of sauce. If not used immediately, float a film of stock or water over the surface to prevent a skin forming. When cold it can be refrigerated for several days or frozen for several weeks.

Variations

Sauce Madère Boil 125 ml (¼-pint) Madeira until it has reduced by half. Add 500 ml (1 pint) of Espagnole Sauce and simmer until the desired consistency is reached. Check the seasoning carefully, take off the heat and beat in 25 g (1 oz) butter in small pieces.
Use for ham, veal, fillet of beef, or egg dishes.

Sauce Périgueux Half way through the cooking of an Espagnole Sauce add 4 tablespoons Madeira and the juice from a 25 g (1 oz) can of truffles. After sieving the sauce at the end of the cooking time add 25 g (1 oz) butter and 2 small very finely chopped truffles.
Use for fillet steaks, ham or veal dishes.

Sauce Chasseur Make an Espagnole Sauce replacing half of the stock with dry white wine, and adding 2 level tablespoons tomato purée. After sieving the sauce add 100 g (4 oz) finely sliced mushrooms sautéed in 25 g (1 oz) butter and a tablespoon of chopped fresh mixed chervil, tarragon and parsley.
Use for chicken, veal or rabbit dishes.

Sauce Hollandaise
Hollandaise Sauce

2 egg yolks
2 teaspoons lemon juice
1 tablespoon water
salt and white pepper
100 g (4 oz) unsalted butter, at room temperature

Put the egg yolks, lemon juice, water and a pinch each of salt and pepper into a small basin. Rest the basin over a pan of very hot (but not boiling) water and whisk steadily until the mixture thickens to a cream consistency. Immediately remove from the heat and start adding the butter, 15 g (½-oz) at a time, whisking in each addition until completely absorbed before adding the next. The result should be a sauce of thin mayonnaise consistency, and if necessary it can be thinned down with a few drops of warm water. Take care never to allow this sauce to overheat as it may curdle.

Serve tepid, with asparagus, artichokes, or poached fish or eggs.

Variations

Sauce Mousseline Just before serving fold in 4 tablespoons of lightly whisked double cream.

Sauce Maltaise Stir 1 tablespoon of orange juice and 1 teaspoon of finely grated orange rind into the finished sauce.

Mayonnaise

If you have an electric blender follow the manufacturer's instructions for making the mayonnaise. If mixing by hand, make sure all the ingredients, and the basin, are at room temperature before starting. Put the egg yolks, mustard, salt and a few drops of the vinegar or lemon juice into a small pudding basin and beat thoroughly until the yolks are beginning to thicken, using either a small wire whisk or a wooden spoon for mixing. Start adding the oil drop by drop, beating all the time, until an emulsion is formed; that is to say, the mixture thickens with no signs of separation. Now add half a teaspoon of vinegar or lemon juice and increase the flow of oil to a thin stream, beating all the time. Continue until all the oil is used and the mayonnaise is thick and jelly-like in consistency. If it becomes too thick, beat in a few drops of the vinegar or lemon juice, or plain water. Finally, check the seasoning and beat in the *boiling* water which Francine thought made the sauce beautifully light and creamy. It is also an insurance against separation. Cover the sauce and keep in a cool place, but not the refrigerator, until needed.

2 egg yolks
½ level teaspoon made yellow mustard
½ level teaspoon salt
1–2 teaspoons white wine vinegar *or* lemon juice
about 250 ml (½ pint) olive oil *or* ground nut oil, corn oil or a mixture of oils
1 tablespoon boiling water

To Cure a Curdled Mayonnaise

If, in spite of everything, the sauce decides to curdle, stir it, a teaspoonful at a time to start, into either a fresh egg yolk *or* a teaspoon of made mustard. As soon as it has 'taken' again, you can add the rest of the sauce more quickly.

Variations

Sauce Andalouse Beat in 2–3 tablespoons of thick cold Tomato Purée (p. 40) or concentrated purée from a tube. Flavour with a pinch of cayenne and garnish with very thin pieces of fresh or canned sweet red pepper.

Mayonnaise Chantilly Flavour the basic mayonnaise with lemon juice rather than vinegar, and fold in 4 tablespoons of thick fresh cream.

Mayonnaise Collée This is a mayonnaise stiffened for coating cold foods such as chicken, fish and eggs. Dissolve 7 g ($\frac{1}{4}$-oz) powdered gelatine in 2 tablespoons hot water, stir into the mayonnaise and use as soon as it is stiff enough to coat the food.

Mayonnaise Escoffier Add 2 level tablespoons grated horseradish (or more to taste) and 1 tablespoon mixed chopped chervil and parsley.

Sauce Niçoise Stir in 4 level tablespoons of thick cold Tomato Purée (p. 40), 1 crushed clove of garlic, a little finely chopped tarragon and several shakes of paprika.

Sauce Rémoulade Add $\frac{1}{2}$ teaspoon anchovy essence or paste, and $\frac{1}{2}$ tablespoon each of made French mustard, finely chopped gherkin, capers, parsley and chervil.

Sauce Verte Bring 250 ml ($\frac{1}{2}$-pint) water to the boil and add 8 spinach leaves, 25 g (1 oz) watercress, 1 tablespoon each of fresh tarragon, parsley, and spring onions. Boil for 3 minutes, then drain and dry. Press through a sieve and stir the purée into the mayonnaise. If making the mayonnaise in an electric blender, put the cooked leaves into the goblet with the egg yolks and seasoning.

Sauce à la Moutarde
Mustard Sauce

2 egg yolks
1 level tablespoon yellow French mustard
salt and ground black pepper
65–125 ml ($\frac{1}{8}$–$\frac{1}{4}$ pint) vegetable oil
1 teaspoon wine vinegar

Put the egg yolks, mustard, salt and pepper into a basin and mix thoroughly. Rest the basin over a saucepan of hot but not boiling water, and add the oil drop by drop, beating continuously, as for a mayonnaise. When the sauce thickens, which it will do quite quickly, remove from the heat and add the oil a teaspoon at a time, still beating continuously, until you have the required amount of sauce. Then, as necessary, add a few drops of vinegar and adjust the seasoning.

Serve with grilled steaks, chops, herring or mackerel.

Sauce Nantua
Nantua Sauce

Roughly chop the scampi or prawns. Melt the butter in a saucepan, add the scampi and heat through gently, stirring frequently. When hot, pour the brandy into a heated spoon, light it and pour flaming over the fish. Shake the pan gently. When the flame has gone out, stir in the cream, Béchamel Sauce and, little by little, the shellfish butter. Season to taste.

Serve with poached turbot, halibut or sole.

12 scampi or large prawns, cooked and shelled
50 g (2 oz) butter
2 tablespoons brandy
2 tablespoons double cream
250 ml (½ pint) coating Béchamel sauce (p. 33)
50 g (2 oz) shellfish butter (p. 35)
salt and pepper

Sauce au Paprika
Paprika Sauce

Chop the onion very finely then cook *very gently* in 40 g (1½ oz) of melted butter for about 10 minutes until translucent, but not beginning to colour. Stir in the flour and about half of the paprika, and cook, stirring, for 2 minutes. Take off the heat and stir in the stock smoothly, by degrees. Add the thyme, bay leaf and salt and pepper, and bring slowly to the boil, stirring all the time. Simmer for several minutes then press the sauce through a sieve. Return to the pan and reheat slowly. Just before serving, and off the heat, stir in the cream, lemon juice, the remaining butter, and more paprika if necessary—the sauce should be a pretty pink. Check the seasoning.

Francine used to say that Paprika Sauce was delicious with steamed chicken, almost any fish, and most hot egg dishes.

1 small onion, peeled
45 g (1¾ oz) butter
3 level tablespoons flour
1 level teaspoon paprika
375 ml (¾ pint) chicken stock
1 small sprig thyme
¼ bay leaf
salt and white pepper
3 tablespoons double cream
juice of half a lemon

Sauce aux Crevettes
Shrimp Sauce

Wipe but do not peel the mushrooms. Melt the butter in a saucepan and fry the mushrooms until they have given out their liquid, then drain and chop them. Stir the tomato purée into the Béchamel Sauce and simmer over low heat for 10 minutes. Add the chopped mushrooms, shrimps and seasoning to taste, and heat for a minute. Stir in the cream just before serving.

Francine held that this was superb for any hot fish dish.

200 g (8 oz) button mushrooms
25 g (1 oz) butter
2 level tablespoons concentrated tomato purée
500 ml (1 pint) coating Béchamel Sauce (p. 33).
100 g (4 oz) shelled shrimps
salt and pepper
2 tablespoons double cream

Sauce Robert
Brown Mustard Sauce

Finely chop the onion. Heat the oil in a heavy saucepan and cook the onion very gently for 5 minutes, until soft but not browned. Add the wine or vermouth and boil briskly until reduced to about 2 tablespoons. Stir in the Espagnole Sauce

25 g (1 oz) onion, peeled
1 tablespoon oil
125 ml (¼ pint) dry white wine *or* 4 tablespoons dry vermouth
250 ml (½ pint) Espagnole Sauce (p. 36)
2 level tablespoons French mustard
50 g (1 oz) butter
2 tablespoons chopped parsley

salt and pepper

and simmer gently for 10 minutes. Take off the heat, and just before serving, beat in the mustard, butter and parsley, and check the seasoning.

Serve with grilled chicken, pork chops, or *réchauffée* meat.

Coulis de Tomates
Fresh Tomato Purée

2 tablespoons oil
1 small onion, peeled
1 small clove garlic, peeled
1 shallot, peeled
450 g (1 lb) ripe tomatoes
1 sprig thyme
½ bay leaf
salt and ground black pepper
a little sugar
ground cumin seeds (optional)

Heat the oil slowly in a heavy based saucepan. Chop the onion, garlic and shallot, add to the oil and cook gently, covered, over very low heat, for about 10 minutes, until almost translucent. Chop the tomatoes roughly, and add to the pan with the thyme, bay leaf and a little salt and pepper. Cook very gently, uncovered, for about 30 minutes or until reduced to a pulp. Pass the sauce through the fine mesh of a vegetable mill or nylon sieve, check the seasoning, add sugar and cumin if used, to taste. Reheat, and if too thin boil rapidly, uncovered, until reduced to the required consistency. This is a good sauce to serve with egg, vegetable, chicken, or pasta dishes.
Note If reduced to a thick purée this Coulis de Tomates is used for flavouring other sauces such as mayonnaise.

Sauce Soubise
Onion Sauce

200 g (8 oz) onions, peeled
40 g (1½ oz) butter
1½ level tablespoons flour
250 ml (½ pint) boiling milk *or* veal stock
salt and white pepper
pinch grated nutmeg
2 tablespoons double cream

Slice the onions thinly. Melt the butter in a thick saucepan, add the onions and cook very gently, covered, for 15–20 minutes, until tender but not browned. Add the flour and stir over low heat for 2 minutes. Take off the heat and stir in the milk or stock, and then simmer gently for 10–15 minutes, stirring now and then. Purée in an electric blender or press through a sieve. Add salt, pepper and nutmeg to taste. Reheat, adding the cream, and a little more milk or stock if the sauce has become too thick.

Serve with poached eggs, chicken, veal or mutton, or as a coating for vegetables to be gratinéed.

Sauce Vinaigrette
French Dressing

2 tablespoons wine vinegar
¼ level teaspoon dry mustard
⅛ level teaspoon salt
large shake white pepper
6 tablespoons olive oil *or* vegetable oil

Place all the ingredients in a screw top jar and shake vigorously until well blended. Shake again immediately before using. Makes about 125 ml (¼-pint).
Vinaigrette aux Herbes Just before using stir in 1–2 tablespoons chopped mixed fresh herbs, e.g. parsley, chives, tarragon.

Les Hors d'Oeuvre
et les Salades
Hors d'Oeuvres and Salads

An hors d'œuvre is a customary start to a midday meal in France. In the home this is usually a single dish such as a pâté, quiche, vinaigrette dressed vegetable, a salad or an egg dish. Or it may be a simple mixture of ingredients such as tuna fish, garlic sausage, black olives and crisp radishes. The whole purpose of an hors d'œuvre is to introduce the meal and stimulate the appetite, so the ingredients should be fresh and of fine quality, and the arrangement simple but colourful.

Soufflés

Although soufflés are usually served in the mould in which they were cooked, they can be turned out and covered, and surrounded with a sauce. Any of the following recipes can be served in either way but the cooking is slightly different. Soufflés to be served in the mould are put direct into a hot oven, while those to be unmoulded are set in a baking tin half full of hot, not boiling, water. The temperature can be raised a little for the last few minutes but the water in the baking tin must never boil.

Editor's note A steamed soufflé does not rise quite so much and has a slightly firmer texture which holds its shape well after unmoulding. It doesn't suffer if it has to be kept waiting; simply turn off the heat and leave the soufflé in its water bath. Unmoulded soufflés can be cooked in a metal Charlotte mould or in a china soufflé case.

Champignons à la Grecque
Mushrooms in Oil and Lemon Juice

For this recipe the mushrooms need to be really fresh and firm. Wash and drain them; leave whole if they are small, but if large cut them into quarters. Put all the remaining ingredients into a stainless steel or enamel-lined saucepan and simmer gently for 10 minutes. Add the mushrooms and cook gently for 6–7 minutes, shaking or stirring frequently to cook evenly. Lift out the mushrooms with a perforated spoon and arrange in a shallow serving dish. Boil the liquid rapidly, uncovered, until reduced to about 4–5 tablespoons, then strain over the mushrooms. Serve cold on their own, or as part of a mixed hors d'œuvre.

450 g (1 lb) fresh button mushrooms
250 ml (½ pint) water
4 tablespoons olive oil
4 tablespoons lemon juice
½ level teaspoon salt
2 tablespoons chopped shallots
1 small bay leaf
1 small sprig thyme
6 coriander seeds
8 peppercorns
pinch celery or fennel seeds

Serves 4

Ratatouille au Fenouil
Fennel Ratatouille

Francine recommended that this should be served in the earthenware dish in which it is cooked. It is safer to set it on an asbestos mat (or cook it in a heavy based casserole).

Discard any discoloured parts from the fennel and halve the bulbs lengthways. Finely slice the onions, roughly chop the tomatoes and slice the courgettes. Heat the oil in a heavy based casserole and sauté the onions very gently until translucent. Arrange the fennel on the onions and cover with the tomatoes and courgettes. Add the thyme, bay leaf, clove and salt and pepper to taste. Cover the dish and cook over the lowest possible heat for 1 hour or until all the vegetables are tender. Uncover the dish, increase the heat and let the juice evaporate and reduce—if necessary you may have to spoon some out as the finished ratatouille should be moist but not sloppy. Sprinkle with chopped parsley before serving. This dish can be eaten cold or hot.

450 g (1 lb) fennel bulbs
200 g (8 oz) onions, peeled
450 g (1 lb) ripe tomatoes, peeled
2 courgettes
3 tablespoons olive oil
1 small sprig thyme
½ bay leaf
1 clove
salt and ground black pepper
1 tablespoon chopped parsley

Serves 3 or 4

Maquereaux au Vin Blanc
Mackerel in White Wine

Ask the fishmonger to remove the heads and clean the mackerel. Generously butter a shallow ovenproof dish into which they will fit fairly closely. Thinly slice the carrot and onions and scatter over the bottom of the dish with the bay leaf and lemon slices. Arrange the mackerel on top, head to tail and side by side in a single layer. Season with salt and pepper and pour the wine over them. Cook in a preheated moderately hot oven 190°C 375°F or Gas Mark 5 for 20 minutes, basting several times. Leave to cool in the liquid. Serve sprinkled with fresh herbs.

6 small fresh mackerel
15 g (½ oz) butter for greasing
1 medium carrot, scraped
2 small onions, peeled
1 small bay leaf
3 slices lemon
salt and ground black pepper
300 ml (generous ½ pint) dry white wine
1 tzblespoon chopped herbs—parsley, chervil and chives, as available

Serves 6

Œufs Farcis Andalouse
Eggs Stuffed with Andalouse Sauce

6 large hard-boiled eggs
150 g (6 oz) shelled shrimps
4 heaped tablespoons stiff Andalouse Sauce (p. 38)
125 ml (¼ pint) plain Mayonnaise (p. 37)

Serves 4

Shell the eggs and cut them in half lengthways with a very sharp knife. Take the yolks out carefully and set them aside. Mix 50 g (2 oz) of the shrimps into the Andalouse Sauce and stuff eight of the egg whites with it. Mix the remaining shrimps with the plain mayonnaise, and if necessary reduce to a coating consistency with a few drops of water. Arrange six of the egg yolks, rounded end up, in the centre of a circular serving dish and coat with the mayonnaise and shrimps. Put three egg yolks on top, coat with more mayonnaise and set the remaining three yolks on top again. Arrange the eight stuffed whites round the edge of the dish. Chop the remaining whites and spoon round the mound of yolks in the centre.

Figues au Jambon de Parme
Parma Ham with Green Figs

8 very thin slices raw Parma ham
12 fresh green figs

Serves 4

Roll the slices of ham and arrange them around a dish with the figs in the centre. The combination of ham and fruit is delicious.

Celeri-rave Rémoulade
Celeriac with Mustardy Mayonnaise

1 young celeriac, about 400 g (scant 1 lb)
2 teaspoons lemon juice
salt
about 1 teaspoon yellow French mustard
125 ml (¼ pint) mayonnaise (p. 37)
1 tablespoon chopped parsley

Serves 3 or 4

Peel the celeriac coarsely. Cut the flesh into very thin slices and then into matchsticks of about 2½ cm (1 inch) long. As soon as prepared, drop immediately into ice cold water acidulated with the lemon juice. When all are ready, drain, plunge into boiling salted water and cook for just 2 minutes; drain and cool. Stir enough French mustard into the mayonnaise to give it a pronounced mustard flavour. Add the cold celeriac and combine gently. Pile into a dish and sprinkle with parsley. Serve soon after preparation; so that the celeriac retains its crispness, either alone or as part of a mixed *hors d'œuvre*.

Salade de Riz, Petits Pois et Crevettes Roses
Rice, Pea and Prawn Salad

150 g (6 oz) long grain rice
salt
200 g (8 oz) shelled peas, fresh or frozen
150 g (6 oz) picked prawns or shrimps
250 ml (½ pint) Mayonnaise (p. 37)
2 firm ripe tomatoes, quartered

Serves 6

Cook the rice in plenty of boiling salted water until just firm (about 15 minutes) then drain and dry. Cook the peas according to kind, drain and cool. When cold, mix the rice, peas, prawns or shrimps, add the mayonnaise and mix thoroughly. Pile into a serving dish, and arrange the quartered tomatoes around the base. If a few whole prawns are available arrange these between the tomatoes as a garnish.

44

Salade de Francine
Francine's Fennel Salad

About 1 hour before serving, remove any discoloured outer leaves of fennel and cut the roots vertically into *thin* slices. Wash them in iced water, drain and shake in a clean cloth until quite dry. Put the vinaigrette in a salad bowl, add the fennel and toss it, then pile it up in the middle of the bowl and leave for at least half an hour. Meanwhile, shell the hard-boiled eggs and cut lengthways in half. Remove the yolks, mash them and stir in enough mayonnaise to make a very stiff sauce. Stuff the whites with this sauce. Cut each slice of ham into two or three pieces, arrange around the fennel and set the eggs on the ham. Sprinkle alternate eggs with the chopped herbs.

4 good fennel roots
4–6 tablespoons Vinaigrette Dressing (p. 40)
6 hard-boiled eggs
about 125 ml (¼ pint) Mayonnaise (p. 37)
6 thin slices Parma ham
1 heaped tablespoon chopped chervil *or* parsley

Serves 6

Medaillons Farcis de Foie Gras
Foie Gras Medallions in Aspic

Cut the foie gras into six equal slices and sandwich each between two slices of galantine. Arrange flat and not touching each other in a shallow dish. Cut the truffles (if used) into six slices and put one on top of each medallion. When the aspic is cold and on the point of setting, pour a little carefully over each medallion, and put the dish in the refrigerator to set. Repeat this several times until the medallions are well coated.

To serve, cut the medallions out of the surrounding aspic and arrange them on a serving dish. Chop all the left-over aspic and arrange around them. Garnish with the tomatoes and the parsley.

200 g (7–8 oz) can roulade de foie gras truffée
12 thin round slices galantine
25 g (1 oz) can truffles (optional)
250 ml (½ pint) aspic jelly
6 firm ripe tomatoes, skinned and quartered
sprigs of parsley

Serves 6

Ratatouille Glacée
Iced Ratatouille

Peel the aubergines and cut into 1½ cm (¾-inch) dice. Wipe the courgettes and cut across into 1 cm (⅓-inch) slices. Sprinkle both lightly with salt and leave to drain in a colander for at least half an hour. Peel and slice the onions. Halve, de-seed and finely slice the peppers. Peel and crush the garlic and skin and slice the tomatoes. Heat the oil in a wide, heavy pan and fry the onion gently until soft. Add the aubergines, courgettes, peppers and garlic. Stir well, then cover and cook very gently for 20–30 minutes. Add the tomatoes and continue cooking gently for another 30 minutes or until all the vegetables are soft. At this stage, if the ratatouille looks too liquid, uncover and allow the excess liquid to evaporate. Check the seasoning, turn into a covered dish, and when cool refrigerate until needed.

200 g (8 oz) aubergines
200 g (8 oz) courgettes
salt
200 g (8 oz) onions
2 sweet peppers
1 clove garlic
450 g (1 lb) tomatoes
5 tablespoons olive oil
chopped fresh herbs*
lemon wedges to garnish
*mixed basil, tarragon, parsley and chives, as available

Serves 4

45

Tomates Fourées au Thon
Tomatoes Stuffed with Tuna Fish

6 large, well shaped tomatoes
salt
198 g (7 oz) can tuna fish
50 g (2 oz) butter
ground black pepper
1 teaspoon Worcestershire sauce or
  few drops of tabasco
bunch of watercress, washed
3 hard-boiled eggs

Serves 6

Choose ripe but firm tomatoes. Cut a slice off the stalk end of each, and with a teaspoon scoop out the pulp. Sprinkle the insides with salt and turn upside down to drain. Turn the tuna fish into a basin and mash with a fork. Add the softened butter and beat to a cream with seasonings of pepper and sauce. Pile into the tomato cases. To serve, arrange the tomatoes on a bed of watercress sprigs with halved eggs in the centre.

Foies de Volailles en Gelée
Chicken Livers in Aspic

200 g (8 oz) chicken livers
30 g (1 oz) butter
1 shallot, peeled and halved
salt and ground black pepper
250 ml (½ pint) aspic jelly crystals
250 ml (½ pint) hot water *less* 3
  tablespoons
3 tablespoons medium dry sherry *or*
  Madeira
6 pieces fresh toast, about 5 cm (2
  inches) square
sprigs parsley to garnish.
Rémoulade Sauce (p. 38) to serve
  (optional)

Serves 6

Wash the chicken livers, remove any discoloured parts and cut into pieces roughly equal in size. Heat the butter in a small pan, add the shallot and the livers. Fry gently for 6–8 minutes, turning frequently, until just cooked but still slightly pink in the centre. Discard the shallot, season, and leave to become cold. Dissolve the aspic crystals in the water and then stir in the sherry or Madeira; leave to cool. Divide the livers among the pieces of toast and stand on a wire rack over a baking sheet. When the aspic is on the point of setting, coat the livers and leave to set. Repeat once more. Chill any remaining jelly and then chop it finely. Serve the pieces of toast garnished with parsley and chopped jelly. Serve the sauce separately.

Poireaux à la Niçoise
Leeks with Oil and Tomatoes

8 small leeks
4 tablespoons olive oil
salt and ground black pepper
450 g (1 lb) ripe tomatoes, skinned
  and chopped
1 clove garlic, peeled and crushed
1 tablespoon chopped parsley

Serves 4

Trim the leeks, and wash very thoroughly in cold water to remove all traces of grit. Dry them carefully. Heat the oil in a large, thick based pan, put in the leeks, side by side, and sprinkle them with salt and pepper. Cover, and cook over *very low* heat for 15–25 minutes, or until tender, turning them once. Lift out and arrange in a shallow serving dish. Add the tomatoes and garlic to the oil remaining in the pan and cook for a few minutes. Stir in the parsley and pour over the leeks. Serve cold.

Citrons Fourés
Sardine Stuffed Lemons

6 medium lemons
120 g (4¼ oz) can sardines in tomato
sauce
100 g (4 oz) butter
1 level teaspoon French mustard
2 level teaspoons paprika
paper-thin slices of bread and butter

Serves 6

Cut a good slice off the stalk end of each lemon. Scoop out the pulp, chop it and set aside with the juice. Remove the backbones and tails of the sardines and mash them with their sauce. Soften the butter if necessary, beat to a cream, add the sardines, mustard, lemon pulp and juice and 1 teaspoon of paprika; mix thoroughly. Stuff the lemons with this mixture and then refrigerate for at least half an hour.

To serve, stand the lemons in egg cups or small glasses. Dust the bread and butter with paprika and arrange around the lemons.

Riz Gitane
Gipsy Rice

Boil the rice in plenty of boiling salted water with the thyme, bay leaf and saffron, if used. When just tender—this will take from 15–20 minutes according to variety—drain, discard the herbs, and put the rice into a large salad bowl. Add the carrots, peas, raw mushroom caps, and the green and black olives.

Cut the eggs in half, remove the yolks, chop the whites and add to the salad.

Put the yolks and anchovy fillets into a small basin and pound to a cream. Gradually stir in the olive oil, and then the vinegar, paprika and a few shakes of pepper. Pour this sauce over the rice and vegetables and toss everything well. Check the seasoning and serve very cold.

200 g (8 oz) long grain rice
salt
1 sprig thyme
1 bay leaf
2–3 pinches saffron (optional)
3 carrots, cooked and diced
200 g (8 oz) peas, cooked
200 g (8 oz) button mushrooms, washed and dried
6–8 pitted green olives
6–8 pitted black olives
2 hard-boiled eggs
4 anchovy fillets in oil
6 tablespoons olive oil
2 tablespoons wine vinegar
1–2 pinches paprika
ground black pepper

Serves 6

Salade de Bananes et Laitue
Banana and Lettuce Salad

Wash the lettuce leaves, pat dry, put into a plastic bag and leave in the refrigerator to crisp. Peel the bananas, cut across in thinnish slices, sprinkle with salt, pepper, paprika and 1 tablespoon of lemon juice. Toss lightly and leave for 15 minutes. Peel the orange and divide into sections removing all pith and pips. Mix the remaining lemon juice with the cream and season with salt, pepper and cayenne.

Line a salad bowl with the lettuce leaves, pile the banana slices and orange sections in the centre and top with the cream dressing.

1 large lettuce
3–4 ripe, firm bananas
salt and ground black pepper
½ level teaspoon paprika
1½ tablespoons lemon juice
1 orange
125 ml (¼ pint) double cream
pinch cayenne pepper

Serves 4

Escargots à la Niçoise
Snails with Anchovies

Pound the anchovy fillets and butter to a paste. Put the oil, garlic, thyme and bay leaf into a saucepan, cover, and leave over the lowest possible heat for 15 minutes or until the oil is well flavoured. Remove the garlic and herbs.

Drain the snails thoroughly, put into the flavoured oil, stir

6 anchovy fillets
65 g (2½ oz) butter
5 tablespoons olive oil
1 clove garlic, peeled and quartered
1 sprig thyme
½ bay leaf
1 can containing 36 snails
36 snail shells

Serves 6

well, cover the pan and leave over a very low heat for 5–10 minutes. One by one, remove the snails from the oil and put each into a snail shell, pushing it down and then filling the shell with a little anchovy butter. Stand the shells open end upwards, in the snail dishes, and dribble a few drops of oil over them. Transfer carefully to a hot oven preheated to 200°C, 400°F or Gas Mark 6 for 5–8 minutes. Serve at once, keeping the dishes steady to retain the butter in the shells.

Canapés de Bananes
Banana and Cheese Canapés

4 ripe bananas
1 tablespoon rum
salt and ground black pepper
4 large slices bread
a little butter
4 thin slices Gruyère cheese, slightly smaller than the bread
paprika

Serves 4

Mash the bananas to a pulp with the rum and a sprinkling of salt and pepper. Remove the crusts and butter the bread on one side. Spread with the mashed bananas. Place on a baking sheet and put in a moderate oven preheated to 180°C, 350°F or Gas Mark 4 for 10–12 minutes, until heated through and beginning to bubble. Cover with a slice of cheese and put back in the oven for another 5 minutes, until melted. Dust with a very little paprika and serve at once.

Foie Gras Flambé
Foie Gras with Armagnac

325 g (12 oz) can roulade de foie gras truffée
6 small slices of bread, 1 cm (⅓ inch) thick
75 g (3 oz) unsalted butter
4 tablespoons Armagnac* *or* brandy

Serves 6
*Armagnac is a brandy from a particular district

Cut the foie gras into six equal slices. Remove the crusts and cut the bread into neat squares a little larger than the pieces of foie gras. Heat 50 g (2 oz) of the butter in a frying pan and fry the bread lightly on each side. While still hot spread with the rest of the butter and arrange on a hot flameproof dish. Put a slice of foie gras on each slice of fried bread. Heat the brandy just to boiling point, pour it over the foie gras, light it, and serve immediately while still aflame.

Œufs sur Canapés
Eggs on Canapés

4 small slices of bread for toasting
4 small, thin slices cooked ham
4 small, thin slices Gruyère cheese
a little butter
4 fresh eggs
salt and white pepper

Serves 4

Using a 7½ cm (3 inch) round cutter, cut four circles of bread, four circles of ham and four of Gruyère. Toast the bread, spread lightly with butter, cover with the ham and top with the cheese. Arrange on a baking tray. Carefully separate the yolks and whites of the eggs, keeping the yolks whole. Beat the whites to a stiff foam with a little salt and pepper. Spread over the cheese forming hollows in the centre, and drop the egg yolks into the hollows. Bake in the centre of a moderately hot oven preheated to 190°C, 375°F or Gas Mark 5 for 5–8 minutes, until lightly set. Serve immediately.

Paupiettes de Jambon aux Bananes
Ham and Banana Rolls

Peel the bananas and dust them with salt, pepper and paprika. Roll each one in a slice of ham. Butter an ovenproof dish into which the paupiettes can be fitted fairly closely. Sprinkle the cheese over them, dot with the remaining butter and pour the cream evenly over all. Bake in the upper half of a hot oven pre-heated to 200°C, 400°F or Gas Mark 6 for about 20 minutes, until the bananas are soft and the surface golden. May be served either hot or cold.

6 bananas
salt and ground black pepper
paprika
6 thin slices cooked ham
25 g (1 oz) butter
50 g (2 oz) Parmesan cheese, grated
125 ml (¼ pint) double cream

Serves 6

Canapés de Saumon
Scrambled Egg and Salmon Toast

Butter a plate and a piece of greaseproof paper to cover it, and heat the plate over a saucepan of boiling water. Place the salmon on the plate, cover with the paper and the saucepan lid. Steam the fish for 15–20 minutes, turning it over when half cooked. Drain the salmon, discard any skin and bone, flake the fish roughly and keep hot over the saucepan. Toast the bread and butter it. Beat the eggs and season with salt and pepper. Melt the remaining butter in a heavy saucepan, add the eggs and stir over gentle heat until lightly scrambled. Stir in the cream. Divide the eggs among the pieces of toast, then top with the salmon. Serve immediately.

55 g (generous 2 oz) butter
200 g (8 oz) cutlet fresh salmon
6 slices crustless bread
10 eggs
salt and ground black pepper
2 tablespoon single cream

Serves 6

Champignons Farcis
Stuffed Mushrooms

Choose even-sized 'cup' shaped mushrooms, *not* flat ones. Wash and drain. Remove the stalks and chop them. Finely chop the onions, shallots and garlic. Wash the livers and chop them separately. Heat 25 g (1 oz) of the butter and the oil in a wide pan and fry the mushroom caps gently for a few minutes until beginning to soften, then drain and arrange cup side up in an ovenproof dish. Meanwhile heat the remaining butter in a saucepan and fry the onions, shallots and garlic over *low* heat for 5 minutes or until soft, then add the mushroom stalks and chicken livers and fry for another 5 minutes, stirring frequently. Take off the heat and stir in the well beaten eggs, the cream, cayenne, nutmeg and seasoning. Heat gently, stirring continuously until lightly set. Pile into the mushroom caps and serve at once. Alternatively, after the addition of the raw eggs, spoon the mixture into the mushroom caps and put into a preheated moderate oven 180°C, 350°F or Gas Mark 4 for 7–10 minutes or until lightly set. Serve alone as an *hors d'œuvre*, or as an accompaniment to roast chicken or game.

12 large open 'cup' mushrooms
2 medium sized onions, peeled
2 shallots, peeled
1 clove garlic, peeled
100 g (4 oz) chicken livers
75 g (3 oz) butter
1 tablespoon oil
2 eggs
1 tablespoon double cream
pinch cayenne
pinch grated nutmeg
salt and ground black pepper

Serves 6

Œufs au Lit
Eggs in Tomatoes

4 round, ripe, firm tomatoes
salt and pepper
2 tablespoons oil
4 slices bread
50 g (2 oz) butter
4 small eggs
1 tablespoon chopped parsley

Serves 4

Cut a slice off the stalk end of each tomato, and with a teaspoon carefully scoop out the seeds and pith. Sprinkle the insides with salt and pepper and turn the tomatoes upside down to drain. Leave for at least 15 minutes. Heat the oil in a saucepan, put in the tomatoes (hollow side up), cover, and cook *very gently* for 5 minutes. Meanwhile remove the crusts from the bread and cut into neat squares. Fry quickly in the butter so that the bread remains soft, then arrange on a baking tray and set a tomato on each. Season the insides of the tomatoes and carefully drop an egg into each. Cook in a moderately hot oven preheated to 190°C, 375°F or Gas Mark 5 for 6–8 minutes. The whites should be set but the yolks remain runny. Sprinkle with salt and chopped parsley, and serve immediately.

Œufs Brouillés Vancouver
Scrambled Eggs with Smoked Salmon

150 g (6 oz) smoked salmon
8 eggs
salt and ground black pepper
7 tablespoons double cream
50 g (2 oz) butter
fingers of toast to garnish

Serves 4

Cut half of the salmon into neat pieces for garnishing, and reserve. Chop the remainder. Beat the eggs with a little salt and pepper, and 1 tablespoon of the cream. Melt the butter in a heavy saucepan, add the eggs and chopped salmon, then stir with a wooden spoon over low heat until gently scrambled: the mixture must remain creamy. Immediately remove from the heat and divide among four small serving dishes. Bring the remaining cream to the boil, pour it over the eggs and arrange the pieces of reserved salmon on top. Garnish with the fingers of toast.

Paupiettes de Jambon Fourées aux Champignons
Mushroom-Stuffed Ham Rolls

2 brioches
125 ml (¼ pint) hot milk
100 g (4 oz) firm mushrooms, washed
30 g (generous 1 oz) butter
2 eggs, well beaten
100 g (4 oz) Gruyère cheese, grated
salt and ground black pepper
6 thin slices cooked ham

Serves 6

Put the brioches in a basin, pour the milk over them, and let them stand for 10 minutes. Drain them, squeeze them in your hands to press out any remaining milk, and then mash them to a purée. Finely chop the mushrooms, then sauté them in the butter over gentle heat for 10 minutes. Take the pan off the heat and mix in the brioches. Add the eggs, 50 g (2 oz) of the cheese, and salt and pepper to taste. Stir over low heat for about 5 minutes, until the eggs are set, then leave to cool a little. Divide the mixture among the slices of ham, roll up and place side by side in a buttered ovenproof dish. Dust with the remaining cheese and put in a hot oven preheated to 220°C, 425°F or Gas Mark 7 for 10–15 minutes.

Œufs en Cocotte à la Créme
Eggs in Cocotte Dishes with Cream

Set four individual cocotte dishes in a large pan or baking tin. Add hot water to reach half way up the dishes, and place over medium heat until simmering point is reached. Meanwhile, heat the cream just to boiling point, then put 1 tablespoonful into each dish. Break the eggs one by one into a cup and then slide into the dishes. Sprinkle with salt and pepper and spoon the remaining cream over the eggs. Cover the pan and simmer for 4–6 minutes until the whites are lightly set but the yolks still soft. Alternatively, cook in the centre of a moderately hot oven preheated to 190°C, 375°F or Gas Mark 5 for 6–8 minutes. Serve immediately in the dishes.

As a variation sauté a little finely shredded cooked ham, or some chopped mushrooms, in butter and put a spoonful into the bottom of each dish before adding the egg.

125 ml (¼ pint double cream)
4 fresh eggs
salt and ground black pepper

Serves 4

Omelettes au Camembert
Camembert Omelets

Cut the cheese into small cubes. With a fork, beat the eggs lightly with the water and a little salt and pepper. Heat a 15–18 cm (6–7 inch) omelet pan, add a quarter of the butter, and when *just beginning* to turn brown and smell 'nutty' pour in a quarter of the egg mixture. Cook over high heat, shaking the pan gently and lifting the omelet with the fork as it sets to allow the raw egg to run underneath. As soon as it is lightly set, scatter a quarter of the cheese over the surface, fold the omelet in half and turn out on to a serving plate. Repeat until all the cheese and eggs have been used up. The cheese just has time to melt into a delicious creamy filling.

4 single portions Camembert cheese
8 eggs
4 tablespoons cold water
salt and pepper
50 g (2 oz) butter

Serves 4

Croûtes aux Champignons
Mushroom Toast

Wash and dry the mushrooms and cut into thin slices. Melt 25 g (1 oz) of the butter in a saucepan and sauté the mushroom slices gently for about 5 minutes. Add salt and paper, cover the pan and keep warm. Toast the slices of bread and butter them while still warm. Leave a tablespoon or two of the mushrooms in the pan and divide the rest among the slices of toast, spreading them out to cover the surface. Pour a little cream over each and place under a hot grill for a minute or so. Pour the remaining cream into the saucepan with the mushrooms, season to taste, and heat to boiling point. Serve the cream separately.

450 g (1 lb) button mushrooms
about 50 g (2 oz) butter
salt and ground black pepper
6 slices bread for toasting
250 ml (½ pint) double cream

Serves 6

Mousse de Foies de Volaille
Chicken Liver Mousse

125 ml (¼ pint) coating Béchamel
  Sauce (p. 33)
butter for greasing
200 g (8 oz) chicken livers
1 egg
1 egg yolk
salt and ground black pepper
3 tablespoons double cream
1 tablespoon brandy *or* Madeira
about 2 tablespoons thick Tomato
  Purée (p. 40)

Serves 4

Preheat a moderate oven 180°C, 350°F or Gas Mark 4. Make the sauce and leave to cool. Generously butter four cocotte dishes each of 125 ml (¼-pint) capacity. Remove any tissue or discoloured parts from the livers. Put the livers into an electric blender with the egg, egg yolk and salt and pepper to taste, and blend for 1 minute, until smooth. Add the sauce, cream and brandy or Madeira and blend again for a few seconds until mixed. Divide among the cocotte dishes and stand in a baking tin containing very hot water to reach half way up the dishes. Bake in the centre of the oven for 25–30 minutes, until firmly set. Remove from the water, allow to cool for a few minutes then unmould on to small plates. Serve with a teaspoon of Tomato Purée Sauce on each.

Crêpes Gratinées
Baked Pancakes

Basic Pancake Mixture (p. 29)
500 ml (1 pint) very thick Béchamel
  Sauce (p. 33)
150 g (6 oz) grated cheese (p. 21)
salt and white pepper
butter for greasing
250 ml (½ pint) Tomato Sauce (p. 40)
  or thin Béchamel Sauce (p. 33)

Serves 8

Prepare the pancake batter. Make the Béchamel Sauce, add the cheese and seasonings to taste. Prepare fairly thin pancakes, and as they are cooked put a tablespoonful of sauce in the centre of each, roll up and place side by side in a single layer in a buttered, shallow ovenproof dish. When all are ready, coat lightly with the Tomato Sauce, and reheat in the centre of a moderate oven preheated to 180°C, 350°F or Gas Mark 4 for 20 minutes. Alternatively coat with thin Béchamel Sauce, sprinkle thickly with additional grated cheese, then heat through and brown under a moderate grill.

Crêpes aux Moules
Mussel Pancakes

Basic Pancake Mixture (p. 29)
2 litres (3–4 pints) mussels
250 ml (½ pint) dry white wine
1 Bouquet Garni (p. 22)
1 small onion, peeled and chopped
pinch grated nutmeg
ground black pepper
250 ml (½ pint) unpeeled shrimps
75 g (3 oz) soft butter
100 g (4 oz) plain flour
2 teaspoons tomato purée
2 egg yolks
2 tablespoons cream
salt if necessary

Serves 8

Prepare the pancake batter and set aside. Scrape and clean the mussels in several changes of cold water, discarding any that fail to shut tightly when touched. Put into a wide pan with the wine, bouquet garni, onion, nutmeg and pepper. Cover, and cook over brisk heat, shaking the pan frequently, until the mussels open. Remove them from their shells and put in a basin. Peel the shrimps and add to the mussels. Put the shrimp heads and shells into a mortar (a good size one) with 50 g (2 oz) of the butter and the flour, and pound together until well blended. Little by little, blend in the strained mussel stock. Transfer to a saucepan, stir in the tomato purée, and stir until boiling. Simmer for 3 minutes, then pass the sauce through a fine sieve pressing it through with the back of a wooden spoon. Return the sauce to the rinsed saucepan. Make the pancakes, fill each with the mixed mussels and shrimps, roll up and arrange side by side in a buttered ovenproof dish; keep hot in a warm oven. Whisk the egg yolks with the cream, heat up the sauce, then take the pan off the heat and stir it, little by little, into the egg and cream mixture. Beat in the remaining 25 g (1 oz) butter in small pieces. Check the seasoning and pour over the pancakes.

Crêpes au Fromage
Cheese Pancakes

Make the pancake batter and leave to rest. Mash the Brie or Camembert into a paste with the Béchamel Sauce, season to taste, and set aside. Make the pancakes in the usual way and stack them flat. When they are all ready, put the cheese sauce into a saucepan and stir while it heats through. Spread some of this sauce on each pancake, roll them and arrange in a single layer in a buttered ovenproof dish. Dust with grated cheese and set in a moderately hot oven preheated to 190°C, 375°F or Gas Mark 5 to reheat the pancakes and melt the cheese. This will take about 20–30 minutes.

Basic Pancake Mixture (p. 29), half
   quantity
100 g (4 oz) Brie or Camembert
   cheese
4 tablespoons coating Béchamel Sauce
   (p. 33)
salt and ground black pepper
butter for greasing
50 g (2 oz) Parmesan, grated

Serves 4

Pipérade du Pays Basque
Basque Pipérade

Skin the tomatoes, discard the seeds, put the pulp into a colander, sprinkle with salt and leave for half an hour. Slice the peppers lengthways, remove every single seed and cut the flesh into strips. Crush the garlic, and roughly chop the drained tomatoes. Heat 2 tablespoons of the oil in a heavy frying pan and sauté the onion and peppers gently. Before they begin to colour add the garlic and sauté for another minute, then add the tomatoes, salt and pepper and very little sugar. Cook over very low heat until practically all the water has evaporated. Lightly fry the ham in the remaining oil in another pan, then remove the ham and tip its oil in with the tomatoes. Beat the eggs lightly. Take the tomatoes off the stove, stir in the eggs then put the pan back over *low* heat and stir continuously until the eggs have scrambled lightly. Taste and adjust the seasoning, and arrange in a shallow dish with the ham on top. Dust with parsley and serve at once.

Editor's note Francine's original recipe uses 24 small green pickling peppers the size of chillis which, when available should be halved and de-seeded (but not sliced) in the same manner as the green peppers. Mild gammon can be used instead of raw ham.

1 kg (2 lb) ripe tomatoes
salt and ground black pepper
3 sweet green peppers
1 clove garlic, peeled
3 tablespoons oil
1 large onion, peeled and chopped
little sugar
6 small slices raw ham
6 eggs
1–2 tablespoons chopped parsley

Serves 6

Pipérade de Fifine à St. Tropez
Fifine's Pipérade

1 onion
1 clove garlic
1 small green pepper
2 ripe tomatoes
5 or 6 fresh basil leaves *or* ½ teaspoon dried basil
1 tablespoon fresh parsley
½ tablespoon fresh chives
4 eggs
3 tablespoons oil
salt and pepper

Serves 2

This version of pipérade is virtually an omelet. Peel and chop the onion and garlic. Halve, de-seed and finely slice the pepper. Skin and halve the tomatoes, take out the seeds, squeeze the tomatoes in your hands to get out as much water as possible, then cut them into thin slices. Chop the fresh basil, the parsley and chives. Beat the eggs for a full 5 minutes without seasoning. Heat the oil in a heavy frying pan (20 cm or 8 inches in diameter) and fry the onion gently. After a minute or two add the peppers and tomatoes and continue frying for 5–6 minutes, stirring all the time. Add the garlic, basil, parsley, chives and salt and pepper to taste. Increase the heat until the pan is as hot as possible without burning, then pour in the eggs and make an omelet, folding in the vegetables as you lift the edges to let the uncooked egg run underneath. As soon as it is lightly set, fold the omelet and slide it on to the serving dish.

Pipérade Maria
Maria's Pipérade

Ingredients as for Fifine's Pipérade
A few small thin slices of aubergine or courgette

Serves 2

This is a kind of flat omelet, browned on both sides. Put the aubergine or courgette slices in a colander, sprinkle with salt and leave to sweat for 30 minutes. Rinse and pat dry. Prepare exactly as for Fifine's Pipérade, cooking the aubergine or courgette with the peppers and tomatoes. After adding the garlic, basil, parsley, chives and seasoning, turn into a basin and set aside until cold. When ready to cook, heat 2–3 tablespoons oil in a heavy frying pan (20 cm or 8 inches in diameter). Add the well beaten eggs to the vegetables, and when the oil is very hot, put the mixture into the pan and cook like a pancake without stirring, over moderate heat. When just firm, slide it on to a plate, then back into the pan the other way up and cook the other side for 1–2 minutes. Turn out and serve flat.

Quiche Lorraine
Bacon and Cream Flan

200 g (8 oz) Pâté Brisée (p. 30)
100 g (4 oz) streaky bacon rashers
3 eggs
250 ml (½ pint) double cream
freshly ground pepper
grated nutmeg

Serves 4–6

Preheat a hot oven 200°C, 400°F or Gas Mark 6. Roll out the pastry and line a 20 cm (8 inch) diameter flan ring. Line this with greaseproof paper or foil and weight with baking beans or crusts. Bake towards the top of the oven for 10 minutes, then remove the paper and beans. Meanwhile, de-rind the bacon rashers, cut into 2 cm (⅔-inch) strips and simmer in water for 5 minutes; drain and dry. (This is not essential if the bacon is mild.) Fry the bacon lightly in a dry frying pan until the fat begins to run, then sprinkle over the base of the partially cooked flan reserving six or seven pieces for garnishing. Beat the eggs lightly, stir in cream, nutmeg and seasonings, pour over the bacon in the flan. Arrange the reserved pieces of bacon in a star pattern on the surface. Transfer to the top of the oven, lower the heat to 190°C, 375°F or Gas Mark 5 and bake for about 30 minutes until the quiche is puffed up and golden. Serve hot or cold.

Quiche Bourguignonne
Shellfish and Cream Flan

Preheat a hot oven 200°C, 400°F or Gas Mark 6. Line a 20 cm (8 inch) flan ring with the pastry. Line this with greaseproof paper or foil and weight with baking beans or crusts. Bake towards the top of the oven for 10 minutes, then remove the paper and beans. Remove the lobster meat from the shell or can and cut into pieces. Arrange these and the shrimps or prawns in the flan case. Beat the eggs lightly, stir in the cream and seasoning, and pour over the fish. Lower the oven heat to 190°C, 375°F or Gas Mark 5 and bake the flan towards the top of the oven for about 30 minutes. Serve hot or cold, garnished with the unpeeled prawns if available.

200 g (8 oz) Pâté Brisée (p. 30)
1 small lobster *or* 200 g (8 oz) can lobster meat
100 g (4 oz) peeled shrimps *or* prawn
3 eggs
250 ml (½ pint) double cream
salt and pepper
a few unpeeled prawns for garnishing (optional)

Serves 4–6

Soufflé au Fromage
Cheese Soufflé

Well butter a 1 litre (2 pint) capacity soufflé dish. Preheat a hot oven 200°C, 400°F or Gas Mark 6 and a flat baking sheet. Make the Béchamel Sauce in a fairly large saucepan, and when cooked add the cheese and stir until melted. Take off the heat, beat in the egg yolks one by one, and season the mixture fairly generously. In a clean basin, whisk the egg whites until they stand in soft peaks, then fold lightly but thoroughly into the mixture. Immediately turn into the prepared soufflé case, stand on the heated baking sheet and cook in the centre of the oven for 25–30 minutes, until well risen and lightly set. When cut, the soufflé should still be a little creamy in the centre. Serve immediately.

butter for greasing
250 ml (½ pint) very thick Béchamel Sauce (p. 33)
100 g (4 oz) cheese, grated
3 eggs, separated
pinch cayenne pepper
salt and pepper

Serves 3 or 4

Unmoulded Cheese Soufflé
Preheat a moderate oven to 180°C, 350°F or Gas Mark 4. Butter the soufflé mould very generously, especially the base, to facilitate unmoulding. Set the filled soufflé case in a baking tin, and fill the tin with near boiling water to reach half way up the dish. Bake in the centre of the oven until firm (about 45 minutes). Run a flat knife round the soufflé and unmould on to a hot serving dish. Serve covered and surrounded with hot Mornay Sauce (p. 34).

Soufflé au Jambon
Ham Soufflé

Make exactly as for a cheese soufflé but substitute 200 g (8 oz) minced ham for the cheese. If unmoulded, serve with a Tomato Sauce (p. 40).

Soufflé de Volaille
Chicken Soufflé

butter for greasing
200 g (8 oz) cooked chicken*
salt and pepper
4 egg whites
2 egg yolks
125 ml ($\frac{1}{4}$ pint) double cream
250 ml ($\frac{1}{2}$ pint) coating Béchamel
    Sauce (p. 33)
100 g (4 oz) button mushrooms

Serves 3 or 4
*free of all skin, bone and sinews

Well butter a 1 litre (2 pint) soufflé dish. Preheat a moderate oven 180°C, 350°F or Gas Mark 4. Put the chicken through a fine mincer (if you haven't enough cooked chicken make up the weight with mild ham which should also be minced) into a basin. Mix in the seasoning and one egg white, not beaten. Stir in the egg yolks and the cream, mixing thoroughly. Whisk the remaining egg whites until stiff then fold lightly into the mixture. Turn into the mould, set in a baking tin with very hot water to reach half way up the mould, and cook in the centre of the oven until risen and just firm (about 30 minutes). Meanwhile make the Béchamel Sauce, and add the mushrooms —either chopped or whole according to their size. Cover and stand in a larger pan containing near boiling water to keep the sauce hot and to lightly cook the mushrooms. To serve, un-mould the soufflé, pour the sauce over it and serve at once.

Soufflé aux Epinards et Jambon
Spinach and Ham Soufflé

butter for greasing
200 g (8 oz) fresh or frozen spinach
250 ml ($\frac{1}{2}$ pint) very thick Béchamel
    Sauce (p. 33)
100 g (4 oz) cooked ham
3 eggs, separated
salt and pepper

Serves 3 or 4

Well butter a 1 litre (2 pint) soufflé dish. Preheat a hot oven 200°C, 400°F or Gas Mark 6 and a flat baking sheet. Cook the spinach, drain thoroughly, then press it in your hands to squeeze out any remaining water. If necessary chop it finely. Make the Béchamel Sauce in a large saucepan and when cooked beat in the finely minced or chopped ham, the egg yolks, spinach and seasoning to taste. In a clean basin whisk the egg white to the soft peak stage then fold lightly but thoroughly into the mixture. Turn into the prepared soufflé case and bake in the centre of the oven on the hot baking sheet for 25–30 minutes, until well risen and set. Serve immediately.

Unmoulded Soufflé
Cook as for unmoulded Cheese Soufflé (p. 55). To serve, turn out and coat with a 125 ml ($\frac{1}{4}$-pint) of coating Béchamel Sauce enriched with a little cream.

Les Potages

Soups

In most French homes soup is an important part of the evening meal. When it is the first of several courses it will be an elegant soup served in modest portions. But often it is the mainstay of the meal, robust in character and consumed in substantial quantities. In either case it is generally served from a large tureen, and this is what Francine intended. When the soup is to be enriched and thickened with egg yolks and cream, put these directly into the tureen and stir in the boiling soup—with no fear of it overheating and curdling.

For making vegetable purée soups Francine used a mouli-légume (vegetable mill) which speedily produces the slightly rough textured purée characteristic of so many French soups. An electric blender, for all its efficiency, produces a uniformly smooth purée and cannot deal with tough skins, pips or fibres.

Crusty French bread is an essential adjunct to a good soup, and crisp fried croûtons or baked croûtes can provide a welcome crunchy contrast in texture.

Potage Bigourdan
Bigourdan Soup

Wash, peel and chop all the vegetables finely and put them into a saucepan with the water, tomato purée and a little salt and pepper. Bring to the boil, cover, and simmer gently for at least 2 hours. Just before serving the soup, separate the yolk from the white of egg. Whip the white stiffly and put in the bottom of the tureen. Beat the yolk with a tablespoon of cold water, add a little of the hot soup and then stir all back into the pan of soup. Immediately remove from the heat, stir in the butter, adjust the seasoning, and pour the soup into the tureen. The egg white will cook immediately and will rise to the surface coloured pink by the tomato, and making an island in the middle of the vegetables.

200 g (8 oz) tomatoes
100 g (4 oz) turnips
100 g (4 oz) carrots
100 g (4 oz) leeks
100 g (4 oz) potatoes
1 medium onion
1 small stick celery
1 litre (scant 2 pints) water
2 level tablespoons tomato purée
salt and ground black pepper
1 egg
25 g (1 oz) butter

Serves 4 or 5

Soupe Paysanne
Country Soup

Remove bacon rinds and cut the bacon into small dice. Trim the leeks, retaining only the white part, and wash very thoroughly. Chop these finely with the onion and garlic. Cut the potatoes into small cubes. Heat the oil in a large pan, add the bacon and the prepared vegetables and cook over gentle heat for 5 minutes, stirring frequently. Chop the tomatoes and add to the pan with the tomato purée, basil, sugar and a little salt and pepper. Cover, and simmer for about 10 minutes, until you can mash the tomatoes. Add the water, bring to the boil, cover and simmer for 20 minutes. Check the seasoning and add the chervil or parsley at the last minute.

50 g (2 oz) unsmoked streaky bacon
2 small leeks
1 medium onion, peeled
1 clove garlic, peeled
200 g (8 oz) potatoes, peeled
3 tablespoons olive oil
200 g (8 oz) can peeled tomatoes
2 level tablespoons tomato purée
1 or 2 leaves fresh basil
1 teaspoon sugar
salt and ground black pepper
1½ litres (2½ pints) water
chopped fresh chervil *or* parsley to garnish

Serves 6 or 7

Crème de Céleri-rave
Cream of Celeriac

Choose a young celeriac not an old woody one. Peel and roughly chop the celeriac and potatoes. Put them into a saucepan with the water and a very little salt and pepper. Bring to the boil, cover, and simmer for about 30 minutes until the celeriac is soft. Purée the vegetables and the liquid in an electric blender or pass through the fine mesh of a vegetable mill. Return the purée to the pan, add the cayenne, check the seasoning, then bring slowly to the boil. Whisk the egg yolk and cream together lightly in the bottom of a soup tureen. A few minutes before serving, take the soup off the heat and whisk it, a little at a time, into the cream. Serve hot.

300 g (12 oz) celeriac
150 g (6 oz) potatoes
1 litre (scant 2 pints) water
salt and ground black pepper
pinch cayenne
1 egg yolk
5–6 tablespoons cream

Serves 5 or 6

Soupe de Poisson
Fish Soup

1 litre (scant 2 pints) good Fish Stock
  (p. 28)
3 ripe tomatoes
1 large onion
1 shallot
1 small clove garlic
2 tablespoons oil
½ bay leaf
1 small sprig thyme
salt and ground black pepper
pinch saffron
pinch cayenne pepper
garlicky bread Croûtes (p. 21)

Serves 4

Prepare the fish stock ahead, strain and leave to become cold. Peel and finely chop the tomatoes, onion, shallot and garlic. Put into a saucepan with the oil and cook very gently, stirring frequently, for about 15 minutes. Add the bay leaf, thyme and about 250 ml (½-pint) of the fish stock, bring rapidly to the boil, and then pass through the fine mesh of a vegetable mill or sieve. Return the purée to the pan, add the rest of the stock, some salt and pepper, and bring to the boil. Cover, and simmer for 30 minutes. Add the saffron and cayenne, and check the seasoning.

To serve, put the croûtes into a tureen and pour the soup over them, or float one croûte on each plate of soup.

Soupe de Poisson Ghislaine
Ghislaine's Fish Soup

2 leeks
1 onion, peeled
1 shallot, peeled
1–2 cloves garlic, peeled
2 tablespoons olive oil
2 large tomatoes, skinned
thin strip orange peel
1 sprig fennel foliage
1 sprig thyme
1 small bay leaf
salt and ground black pepper
1½ litres (2½ pints) water
1 cod *or* other large fish head, *or*
  several smaller ones
1 pinch saffron
garlicky bread Croûtes (p. 21) to
  accompany

Serves 5 or 6

Trim the leeks and wash very thoroughly in cold salted water. Roughly chop the leeks, onion, shallot and garlic. Heat the oil in a large saucepan, add the chopped vegetables and cook, stirring frequently, until lightly browned. Chop the tomatoes and the orange peel and add to the pan with the herbs, some salt and pepper and the water. Bring to the boil then add the fish heads. Boil gently for 15 minutes. Take the pan off the heat, remove the fish and take out the bones, then pass the fish and vegetables through the finest mesh of a vegetable mill. Combine this purée with the stock in the saucepan, return to the heat, add the saffron and check the seasoning. Serve very hot, with the garlicky bread croûtes.

Soupe Froide aux Poireaux
Iced Leek Soup

450 g (1 lb) leeks
550 g (1¼ lb) floury potatoes, peeled
1 litre (scant 2 pints) chicken stock *or*
  water
salt and ground black pepper
about 6 tablespoons double cream

Serves 6

Trim the leeks, split lengthways and wash very thoroughly. Cut the leeks (both white and all the green part) and the potatoes into rough pieces and put into a pan with the stock or water and a little salt. Cover and simmer until soft, about 30 minutes. Strain the cooking liquid into a basin and reserve it. Purée the potato and leek in an electric blender or pass through the fine mesh of a vegetable mill. Return the purée to the pan and stir in the reserved cooking liquid. Add salt and pepper to taste, and when cold put the soup into the refrigerator to chill for at least 2 hours. Just before serving add the cream, either stirring it into the soup or adding a tablespoonful to each plate.

Crème d'Ail
Cream of Garlic Soup

Peel the potatoes, carrots and garlic and cut them into match-stick pieces. Heat the oil in a saucepan, add the vegetables and cook gently over very low heat for 10 minutes, stirring frequently; the vegetables must not colour. Add the water, thyme, bay leaf and a little salt and pepper (bring to the boil, cover, and simmer very gently for 1½–2 hours. Pass the soup through the fine mesh of a vegetable mill, or remove the thyme and bay leaf and purée in an electric blender. Reheat, and check the seasoning. Put the cream into a tureen and pour the boiling soup on to it.

450 g (1 lb) floury potatoes
150 g (6 oz) carrots
3 cloves garlic
2 tablespoons olive oil
1 litre (scant 2 pints) water
small sprig thyme
½ bay leaf
salt and ground black pepper
2 tablespoons double cream

Serves 4 or 5

Soupe Glacée à la Tomate
Iced Tomato Soup

Scrub the potatoes and boil them in their skins until tender; drain. When cool enough to handle, peel and pass them through the fine mesh of a vegetable mill. Pass the cucumber, shallots and garlic (all uncooked), tomatoes and their juice and basil through the same vegetable mill. Mix them together, stir in the stock or water, tomato purée, sugar and salt to taste. Cover and put the soup into the refrigerator until thoroughly chilled; the soup thickens on standing. Just before serving, add some freshly milled pepper and stir in the cream.

200 g (8 oz) floury potatoes
½ cucumber, peeled
2 small shallots, peeled
1 clove garlic, peeled
200 g (8 oz) can peeled tomatoes
about 8 leaves fresh basil
750 ml (1½ pints) chicken stock *or* water
2 level teaspoons tomato purée
1–2 level teaspoons caster sugar
salt
ground black pepper
1½ tablespoons double cream

Serves 4–6

Crème de Champignons
Cream of Mushroom Soup

Wash the mushrooms but do not peel them. Separate the stalks from the caps, reserve about one third of the smallest caps for garnishing and roughly chop the remainder. Slice the onion. Put the mushroom stalks, chopped mushroom caps, onion, parsley, thyme, bay leaf and water into a saucepan and add a level teaspoon of salt and a few grinds of freshly milled pepper. Bring to the boil, cover, and simmer gently for 30 minutes. Pass the soup through the fine mesh of a vegetable mill, or remove the thyme and bay leaf and purée it in an electric blender; return to the saucepan. Mix the cornflour to a cream with 3 tablespoons of cold water, stir into the soup, continue stirring until boiling, then simmer for 5 minutes.

Meanwhile, thinly slice the reserved mushroom caps and sauté quickly for 1 minute in half of the butter. Take the soup off the heat, stir in the lemon juice, remaining butter and the cream. Check the seasoning. Divide the sautéed mushrooms among the serving plates and pour the soup over.

200 g (8 oz) mushrooms
1 medium onion, peeled
2–3 sprigs parsley
1 sprig thyme
½ bay leaf
1 litre (scant 2 pints) water *or* chicken stock
salt and ground black pepper
2 level tablespoons cornflour
50 g (2 oz) butter
1 teaspoon lemon juice
2 tablespoons double cream

Serves 4

Soupe d'Œufs Natalie
Natalie's Egg Soup

1 leek
1 carrot, peeled
½ turnip, peeled
1 litre (1¾ pints) chicken stock
Bouquet Garni (p. 22)
salt and pepper
2 small eggs

Serves 4

Trim the leek and wash it very thoroughly in cold salted water. Roughly chop the leek, carrot and turnip and put into a pan with the cold chicken stock, bouquet garni, and salt and pepper to taste. Bring to the boil, cover, and simmer very gently for about 20 minutes, until the vegetables are tender. Strain the stock and return to the pan without the vegetables. Check the seasoning. Beat the eggs until the whites and yolks are thoroughly mixed. Heat the stock until just short of boiling point, then pour in the egg through a fairly open sieve. Cook, without boiling, for 2–3 minutes only, just until the egg turns into vermicelli-like threads. Grated cheese or croûtons of fried bread (p. 21) go well with this soup.

Soupe à l'Oignon Gratinée
Onion Soup with Cheese Croûtes

450 g (1 lb) onions, peeled
40 g (1½ oz) butter
1 tablespoon oil
2 level teaspoons caster sugar
1¼ litre (2¼ pints) beef *or* chicken
   stock (p. 27)
salt and ground black pepper
4 or 5 slices French bread, 1 cm
   (⅜ inch) thick
butter for spreading
finely grated Gruyère or Parmesan
   cheese

Serves 4 or 5

If large, quarter the onions vertically and then cut into fine slices. Heat the butter and oil in a heavy based pan, add the onions and stir well. Cover and cook very gently for about 10 minutes until soft. Sprinkle with the sugar and continue cooking gently until golden brown. Add the stock and seasoning to taste, and bring to the boil. Cover and simmer gently for 20–30 minutes. Meanwhile, spread the bread with butter and sprinkle lightly with grated cheese. Put one in bottom of each ovenproof soup bowl and pour the boiling soup over. Sprinkle with more cheese and either put into a hot oven until browned, or slip under a hot grill until bubbling and golden. The latter is less authentic but much quicker.

Crème de Petits Pois
Cream of Pea Soup

1 litre (1¾ pints) water
200 g (8 oz) floury potatoes
salt
1 leek
1 small onion, peeled
35 0g (14 oz) can petits pois
1 egg yolk
4 tablespoons double cream
ground black pepper
25 g (1 oz) butter
croûtons of fried bread (p. 21) *or* tiny
   cubes of cooked ham to garnish

Serves 5 or 6

Bring the water to the boil. Peel and cut up the potatoes, and add with 1 teaspoon salt to the boiling water. Trim and thoroughly wash the leek in cold salted water. Chop the white part of the leek and the onion, add to the potatoes and simmer for 25 minutes. Add the contents of the can of peas. Pass the vegetables and water through the finest mesh of a vegetable mill, or purée in an electric blender. Return to the pan, bring to the boil, and simmer for a further 10 minutes or so. When ready to serve whisk the egg yolk, cream and a little pepper together in a soup tureen. Whisk in the hot soup little by little, then taste and adjust the seasoning. Stir in the butter and serve with either the croûtons or ham.

Soupe de Langoustines
Scampi Soup

Twist off the claws, legs and head of the scampi. Cut along the underside of the tail with kitchen scissors and remove the tail meat. Reserve both meat and shells. Finely chop the onion and garlic and roughly chop the tomatoes. Heat the oil in a large saucepan and lightly fry the scampi shells and heads. Add the onion and garlic and fry gently until the onion is lightly browned, then add the tomatoes and some salt and pepper. Cover the pan and simmer very gently for 1 hour. Remove the scampi heads and shells, and pass the rest through the finest vegetable mill, or purée it in an electric blender. Return the purée to the saucepan, add the water and bring to the boil. Add the stock cube, saffron, paprika and cayenne, and simmer for a minute or two, then taste and check the seasoning. Cut the scampi meat into small pieces, add them to the soup and simmer for a few minutes more to heat them through. Serve accompanied by the garlicky bread croûtes.

3 large scampi, cooked but not shelled
1 medium onion, peeled
2 cloves garlic, peeled
550 g (1¼ lb) ripe tomatoes, peeled
2 tablespoons olive oil
salt and ground black pepper
750 ml (1½ pints) water
1 chicken stock cube
pinch saffron
1 level teaspoon paprika
pinch cayenne
Croûtes of garlicky fried bread (p. 21)

Serves 4 or 5

Soupe aux Epinards
Spinach Soup

Wash the fresh spinach in several changes of cold salted water and discard any tough stems or yellowed leaves. Chop roughly. Melt the butter in a large saucepan, add the fresh or frozen spinach and cook gently, stirring now and then, until the fresh spinach has wilted or the frozen spinach thawed. Continue cooking gently, covered, for 5 minutes. Purée the spinach in an electric blender, or pass through the fine mesh of a vegetable mill. Return to the pan, stir in the Béchamel Sauce and cream, and thin to the desired consistency with water, if necessary. Bring just to the boil. Season to taste with salt, pepper and nutmeg. If liked, a poached egg can be served in the centre of each plate, *or* serve the soup sprinkled with chopped hard-boiled egg.

650 g (1½ lb) fresh spinach *or* 450 g (1 lb) frozen spinach
50 g (2 oz) butter
750 ml (1½ pints) pouring Béchamel Sauce (p. 33)
2 tablespoons double cream
a little water, if necessary
salt and ground black pepper
grated nutmeg
poached eggs (optional) *or* 1 hard-boiled egg, chopped

Serves 6

150 g (6 oz) dried haricot or red
  beans
1 small sweet green pepper
200 g (8 oz) potatoes, peeled
1 large onion, peeled
1 clove garlic, peeled
2 tomatoes, skinned
100 g (4 oz) fresh or frozen French
  beans
1 litre (scant 2 pints) water
Bouquet Garni (p. 22)
salt and ground black pepper

For the Pistou
1 ripe tomato, skinned
2 cloves garlic, peeled
1 tablespoon chopped fresh basil or
  1 teaspoon dried
2–3 tablespoons olive oil
grated Parmesan or Gruyère cheese
  to serve

Serves 4–6

Soupe au Pistou
Garlic Flavoured Vegetable Soup

Soak the haricot or red beans overnight in cold water. Next day drain, cover with fresh cold water and simmer until just tender, from 1–2 hours depending on the beans. Drain and reserve. Halve, de-seed and finely chop the pepper. Dice the potatoes and chop the onion, garlic, tomatoes and French beans. Bring the water to the boil in a large saucepan, add all the vegetables including the dried beans, the bouquet garni and salt to taste. Simmer, covered, for about 30 minutes. Remove the bouquet garni and check the seasoning.

Meanwhile make the Pistou. Halve, de-seed and chop the tomato and put into a mortar (or heavy basin) with the chopped garlic and basil. Pound to a paste. When reduced to a paste, beat in the olive oil drop by drop, as for a mayonnaise, until a thick sauce forms. Put this sauce into the tureen and stir in the boiling soup. Serve with grated cheese handed separately.

1 large onion, peeled
200 g (8 oz) potatoes, peeled
50 g (2 oz) butter
salt and ground black pepper
1 litre (1¾ pints) chicken stock
2 bunches watercress
4 tablespoons double cream
2 egg yolks

Serves 6

Crème de Cresson
Watercress Soup

Finely slice the onion and potatoes. Melt the butter in a large saucepan, add the onion and potatoes and fry gently, covered, for about 10 minutes or until the onion begins to soften. Add salt and pepper and the chicken stock. Bring to the boil and simmer for 15 minutes, or until the vegetables are soft. Meanwhile, wash the watercress, reserve some of the best leaves for garnishing and roughly chop the remainder. Add to the soup and simmer for another 5 minutes. Pass the soup through the fine mesh of a vegetable mill or purée in an electric blender. Return to the pan, check the seasoning and bring to the boil. Whisk the cream and egg yolks together in a soup tureen and gradually whisk in the boiling soup. Float the reserved watercress leaves on top, and serve.

1 litre (1¾ pints) good Fish Stock
  (p. 28)
40 g (1½ oz) butter
40 g (1½ oz) flour
1 egg yolk
1 tablespoon double cream
1 tablespoon lemon juice
salt and ground black pepper
75 g (3 oz) peeled shrimps

Serves 5 or 6

Crème aux Crevettes
Cream of Shrimp Soup

Prepare the fish stock ahead, and strain. In a large saucepan melt the butter over a low heat, stir in the flour and cook for a minute or so, then little by little smoothly stir in the fish stock. Bring to the boil, stirring, and simmer for 10 minutes. Just before serving, whisk the egg yolk, cream and lemon juice together in a tureen. Heat the soup, season with salt and pepper, then little by little whisk the hot, but not boiling, soup into the cream mixture. Throw in the shrimps and serve.

Crème de Laitue
Cream of Lettuce Soup

A delicious soup as well as a practical way of using surplus lettuce. Wash, shake dry and roughly shred the lettuce leaves. Finely slice the onion. Melt the butter in a large saucepan, add the onion and lettuce, cover the pan and cook over low heat for 10 minutes. Sprinkle in the flour and cook for another 2–3 minutes, stirring from time to time. By this time the lettuce will have shrunk to a quarter of its original volume. Stir in the stock and salt and pepper to taste, bring to the boil and simmer, covered, for 15 minutes. Sieve the soup or purée it in an electric blender, and return to the pan. Add the cream and heat just to boiling point. Check the seasoning and serve sprinkled with the herbs.

2 large lettuces
1 medium onion, peeled
50 g (2 oz) butter
2 level tablespoons flour
750 ml (1¼ pints) chicken stock
salt and ground black pepper
125 ml (¼ pint) single cream
chopped parsley *or* chervil to garnish

Serves 4

Potage Crécy
Carrot Soup

Choose carrots of a good red colour. Finely slice the carrots, potatoes and onions. Melt 50 g (2 oz) of the butter in a large saucepan, add the vegetables and thyme, and stir well until the vegetables are coated with butter. Cover, and cook over *very low* heat, shaking the pan frequently, for 12–15 minutes. Add the salt, pepper, sugar and water, and bring to the boil. Cover, and simmer for 20–25 minutes, until soft. Pass through the fine mesh of a vegetable mill, or purée in an electric blender. Return to the pan, check the seasoning, and reheat. Just before serving, stir in the remaining butter. Serve sprinkled with herbs, and pass the croûtons separately.

650 g (1½ lb) carrots, peeled
450 g (1 lb) potatoes, peeled
200 g (8 oz) onions, peeled
75 g (3 oz) butter
1 sprig fresh thyme *or* ¼ teaspoon dried
salt and ground black pepper
1 teaspoon sugar
1¼ litres (generous 2 pints) water
chopped chervil *or* parsley to garnish
fried bread Croûtons (p. 21)

Serves 4 or 5

Soupe à l'Oseille
Sorrel and Potato Soup

150 g (6 oz) fresh sorrel
40 g (1½ oz) butter
300 g (12 oz) floury potatoes
1¼ litres (2¼ pints) water
salt and ground black pepper
2 small egg yolks
4 tablespoons milk
Croûtons to serve (p. 21)

Serves 5 or 6

Wash the sorrel, discard any tough stalks and cut the leaves into fine shreds. Melt the butter in a saucepan, add the sorrel and cook gently for a few minutes, until wilted. Meanwhile peel and dice the potatoes. Add to the sorrel with the water and seasoning, and bring to the boil. Cover, and simmer gently for 1 hour. Pass the soup through the fine mesh of a vegetable mill, or purée in an electric blender. Return to the saucepan, check the seasoning and reheat. Beat the egg yolks and milk together in a soup tureen and stir in the boiling soup. Serve the croûtons separately.

Les Légumes

Vegetables

A great deal of care goes into the selection and cooking of vegetables in France. House-wives shop daily for the freshest market produce, always seeking young and tender vegetables, preferably small enough to be cooked whole. The main object in cooking is to conserve flavour and texture. Overcooking or keeping hot is considered a crime. Raw or briefly blanched vegetables are often braised in butter with little or no additional liquid —an excellent method of cooking, but one which demands a heavy-based pan with a tight-fitting lid set over a very low heat. To minimize the risk of 'catching', an asbestos or wire mat is a great help in spreading the heat evenly.

In French homes vegetables, as often as not, are served as a separate course in their own right. Many of Francine's recipes in this chapter are excellent for this purpose, or else they can be served as simple supper dishes.

Fonds d' Artichauts au Fromage
Artichoke Bottoms with Cheese

Drain the artichokes well and arrange in a single layer in a shallow ovenproof dish. Stir the egg yolks and cheese into the cream and add salt and pepper to taste. Pour over the artichokes. Cook in the centre of a preheated slow oven 150°C, 300°F or Gas Mark 2 for 25–30 minutes, or until lightly set. Serve hot.

1 large can artichoke bottoms (10–12 pieces)
2 egg yolks
75 g (3 oz) finely grated Parmesan and Gruyère cheese mixed
250 ml (½ pint) single cream
salt and ground black pepper

Serves 4

Fonds d' Artichauts à la Moelle
Artichoke Bottoms with Bone Marrow

Ask the butcher to saw each of the marrow bones into several pieces. Poach them in gently simmering salted water for 5–6 minutes, then drain and cool a little. Drain the artichoke bottoms and arrange them, hollow side up, on an ovenproof dish. Remove the marrow carefully from the centre of the bones so that it doesn't break up. When cold, cut into fairly thick slices and put 1 slice in each artichoke. Dust lightly with salt and pepper and pour a tablespoon of Bordelaise Sauce on each. Heat through in a preheated hot oven 200°C, 400°F or Gas Mark 6 for 8–10 minutes.

2 marrow bones
salt
1 large can artichoke bottoms (10–12 pieces)
ground black pepper
Bordelaise Sauce (p. 35)

Serves 5 or 6

Aubergines Papeton
Papal Aubergine Pudding

It is said that this recipe was invented by the cook of one of the Avignon popes who compared the local cooking unfavourably with that of Rome. Hence the name 'Papeton'.

Peel the aubergines, cut into slices, sprinkle lightly with salt and leave in a colander to drain for at least 1 hour. When ready to cook, pat the slices dry with a clean tea towel. Finely chop the shallots and garlic. Heat the oil in a heavy based saucepan, put in the aubergines, shallots, garlic, thyme, bay leaf and black pepper to taste. Cover, and simmer very gently, stirring frequently, for 15–20 minutes, or until the aubergines are soft. Purée in an electric blender or pass through a fine sieve. Check the seasoning. Stir in the cream and lightly beaten eggs, and turn into a buttered 1 litre (2 pint) soufflé or pie dish. Cover, and set the dish in a baking tin with hot water to reach half way up the dish. Bake in the upper half of a preheated moderate oven 180°C, 350°F or Gas Mark 4 for 40–50 minutes, until lightly set. Unmould on to a deep dish and pour the tomato sauce over. This is a delicious dish to serve on its own. The time in the oven can be reduced by cooking in individual cocotte dishes.

3 aubergines, about 700 g (1½ lb)
salt
2 shallots, peeled
1 large clove garlic, peeled
3 tablespoons olive oil
1 small sprig thyme
1 small bay leaf
ground black pepper
1 tablespoon double cream
2 large eggs
250 ml (½ pint) Tomato Sauce (p. 40)

Serves 4 or 5

Aubergines 'Chutney'
Purée of Aubergines

450 g (1 lb) aubergines
1 sprig thyme
1 small bay leaf
juice of ½ lemon
powdered ginger
1 tablespoon olive oil
cayenne
salt and ground black pepper
1 small onion, peeled and chopped

Serves 3 or 4

This mildly spiced purée, which goes well with cold meat or fish, would also make a refreshing side dish to serve with curry.

Peel the aubergine, cut each one into four and put into boiling salted water with the thyme and bay leaf. Simmer for 10–15 minutes until very soft. Drain, dry a little by shaking in the pan over gentle heat, then mash to a pulp. Stir in the lemon juice, a large pinch of ginger, olive oil and a shake of cayenne, then season to taste with salt and pepper. Pile into a serving dish and sprinkle with the very finely chopped onion.

Aubergines Farcies
Stuffed Aubergines

3 large aubergines
200 g (8 oz) button mushrooms
1 medium carrot, scraped
1 small stick celery, washed
1 medium onion, peeled
2 slices cooked ham
several sprigs parsley
½ bay leaf
1 sprig *each* thyme and tarragon
salt and ground black pepper
100 g (4 oz) butter
1 tablespoon oil
2 tablespoons dried white breadcrumbs
1 tablespoon lemon juice
parsley sprigs for garnishing

Serves 6

This is one of the best known aubergine recipes of all. Remove the stalks and halve the aubergines lengthways. Prick the flesh deeply with a fork, sprinkle with salt and leave to drain for at least 1 hour.

Wipe the mushrooms and remove the stalks. Mince together (or very finely chop) the mushroom stalks, carrot, celery, onion, ham, parsley, bay leaf, thyme and tarragon leaves. Dry the aubergine halves with kitchen paper, carefully scoop out the pulp (leaving the cases intact) and mash it into the minced ingredients. Add salt and pepper and mix thoroughly. Melt 40 g (1½ oz) of the butter in a frying pan and fry the stuffing gently for about 10 minutes, stirring frequently to brown it all lightly. Pour the oil into an ovenproof dish, add the aubergine cases hollow side up, and put into a preheated hot oven (220°C, 425°F or Gas Mark 7 for 5 minutes. Lower the heat to moderate 180°C, 350°F or Gas Mark 4. Remove the aubergine cases and stuff with the minced mixture. Sprinkle each with breadcrumbs and dot with 40 g (1½ oz) of the butter. Return to the oven and cook for 30–35 minutes. Meanwhile melt the remaining 25 g (1 oz) butter, add the mushroom caps, lemon juice and sprinkling of salt and pepper; sauté for 10 minutes.

To serve, arrange the aubergines on a round dish with their pointed ends to the centre, the mushroom caps between, and sprigs of parsley in the centre.

Courgettes à la Marie
Courgettes in Cream Sauce

Top and tail the courgettes and wipe with a damp cloth. Peel them only if they are large or coarse. Cut into slanting slices, barely 1 cm (⅓-inch) thick. Sprinkle lightly with salt and leave in a colander to drain for an hour. Pat dry in a clean cloth. Heat the butter in a wide, thick based saucepan, add the courgettes and bouquet garni and cook gently, covered, turning from time to time and shaking to prevent sticking, for 12–15 minutes or until tender.

Meanwhile, make the Béchamel Sauce. Take off the heat and whisk in the cream, egg yolk and lemon juice. Check the seasoning, then return to the heat for a minute or two, but do not allow to boil. Pour over the courgettes just before serving.

1 kg (2 lb) courgettes
salt
50 g (2 oz) unsalted butter
1 Bouquet Garni (p. 22)
250 ml (½ pint) pouring Béchamel
  Sauce (p. 33)
3 tablespoons double cream
1 egg yolk
1 tablespoon lemon juice
ground black pepper

Serves 4–6

Les Choux de Bruxelles aux Marrons
Brussel Sprouts with Chestnuts

Make a small incision in the skin of each chestnut, drop into boiling salted water for 5 minutes, then drain. While still hot, peel off the outer and inner skins. Cook the chestnuts in simmering salted water for 30 minutes or until tender. Meanwhile, simmer the bacon in water for 15 minutes, then drain and cut into matchstick strips. Prepare the sprouts. Cook in boiling salted water for 1 minute, drain and rinse in cold water. (This is known as 'refreshing', a process used by the French to enhance the colour of vegetables and remove the strong flavour.) Cook the sprouts in boiling salted water until just tender, about 12–15 minutes. Grill or fry the sausages. Melt the butter and fry the bacon strips until golden. Add the well drained chestnuts and sprouts and heat thoroughly, stirring frequently. Pile in the centre of a shallow serving dish and arrange the sausages around. Check the seasoning.

200 g (8 oz) chestnuts
salt
100 g (4 oz) piece smoked streaky
  bacon
450 g (1 lb) tight firm sprouts
200 g (8 oz) chipolata *or* cocktail
  sausages
50 g (2 oz) butter
ground black pepper

Serves 4

Chou-fleur au Beurre Noir
Cauliflower with Black Butter

Discard any leaves and stalk from the cauliflower, divide it into flowerets, wash in cold salted water and drain. Cook in boiling salted water for 5–6 minutes, until *just* tender, then drain, and keep hot in a shallow serving dish. Meanwhile, heat 40 g (1½ oz) of the butter in a large frying pan and fry the crumbs until crisp and golden, stirring frequently. Scatter the crumbs evenly over the cauliflower. Heat the rest of the butter in the frying pan. As soon as it becomes nut brown take it off

1 large cauliflower
salt
100 g (4 oz) unsalted butter
40 g (1½ oz) dried white breadcrumbs
2 teaspoons wine vinegar
ground black pepper
1 hard-boiled egg to garnish
  (optional)

Serves 4

71

the heat and, holding it well away from you, pour in the vinegar (which will splutter fiercely). Immediately pour over the cauliflower, garnish with the hard-boiled egg, quartered, season and serve at once.

Chou-fleur à la Zita
Cauliflower Zita

1 large cauliflower
salt
75 g (3 oz) butter
3 heaped tablespoons dried white
  breadcrumbs
ground black pepper
250 ml (½ pint) double cream *or*
  coating Béchamel Sauce (p. 33)

Serves 4 or 5

Divide the cauliflower into flowerets, wash in cold water and drain. Drop the flowerets into boiling salted water and cook until *just* tender but not soft, about 5–7 minutes. Meanwhile, heat the butter in a large frying pan and fry the breadcrumbs until crisp and golden; season with salt and pepper. Drain the cauliflower and arrange in a shallow ovenproof dish. Sprinkle with half of the crumbs, pour the cream or Béchamel Sauce over, and dust evenly with the remaining crumbs. Put into a moderately hot oven preheated to 190°C, 375°F or Gas Mark 5 for 10–15 minutes. Serve very hot.

Endives Gratinées au Jambon
Chicory and Ham au Gratin

6 large heads chicory
salt
6 thin slices ham
2 tablespoons double cream
250 ml (½ pint) coating Béchamel
  Sauce (p. 33)
ground black pepper
50 g (2 oz) finely grated Parmesan
  cheese
15 g (½ oz) butter

Serves 6

Cut a slice off the base of each head of chicory, discard any discoloured leaves and wipe the chicory with a damp cloth. Put into a large pan of simmering salted water, and simmer, covered, for 20–25 minutes. Drain very thoroughly. Wrap each piece of chicory in a slice of ham and arrange side by side in a shallow ovenproof dish. Stir the cream into the Béchamel Sauce, check the seasoning, and pour evenly over the chicory. Sprinkle with Parmesan cheese and dot with butter. Cook towards the top of a preheated moderate oven 180°C, 350°F or Gas mark 4 for about 30 minutes, until the sauce is bubbling and golden.

Endives Meunières
Braised Chicory

4 large heads chicory
40 g (1½ oz) butter
1 tablespoon olive oil
1 teaspoon caster sugar
salt and ground black pepper
2 teaspoons lemon juice

Serves 4

Cut a slice from the base of each piece of chicory and remove any discoloured outside leaves. Wipe with a damp cloth if necessary. Heat the butter and oil in a heavy flameproof casserole in which the chicory can lie flat and side by side. When hot, put in the chicory and brown them lightly all over. As they start to colour, sprinkle them with sugar, salt and pepper. When golden brown, cover tightly and cook very *gently* over low heat for 30 minutes or until tender, using a wire or asbestos mat if necessary. When cooked, remove the lid and, if there is any water in the bottom of the casserole, increase the heat until it has evaporated. Sprinkle with lemon juice, transfer to a serving dish and pour the buttery juices over the chicory.

Purée de Lentilles
Lentil Purée

Soak the lentils overnight in cold water. Prepare and roughly chop the carrot and onion. Peel and chop the garlic clove, if used. Drain the lentils and put into a saucepan with fresh water to cover. Add the carrot, onion, garlic if used, bay leaf and 1 teaspoon salt. Bring slowly to the boil, cover, and simmer gently until tender, about 1½ hours (or pressure cook for 15 minutes). When cooked, drain them, and pass them first through the medium and then the finest vegetable mill, or purée in an electric blender. Return to the saucepan, add seasoning to taste and the butter. Stir until well mixed and heated through.

450 g (1 lb) lentils
1 small carrot
1 small onion
1 clove garlic (optional)
1 bay leaf
salt and ground black pepper
50 g (2 oz) butter

Serves 4–6

Kartoffelschnitz
Alsatian Potatoes

Use the yellow-fleshed Dutch potatoes if possible. Peel them thinly, then cut from the middle outwards to make pieces shaped like the segments of an orange. Cook the pieces in gently simmering salted water for 10–12 minutes, or until just tender. Meanwhile, cut the bread into 1 cm (⅓-inch) dice, and fry in 50 g (2 oz) of the butter until crisp. In another 25 g (1 oz) of butter gently fry the onion until soft and beginning to turn golden. As soon as the potatoes are cooked, drain and put into a hot vegetable dish. Add the remaining butter to the onion, and when melted add the bread croûtons and tip everything over the potatoes. Serve very hot.

550 g (1¼ lb) waxy potatoes
salt
1 large slice bread, 1 cm (⅓ inch) thick
100 g (4 oz) butter
75 g (3 oz) onion, finely chopped
Croûtons to serve (p. 21)

Serves 3 or 4

Pommes de Terre Rissolées
Golden Potatoes

If the potatoes are fresh wash them well, then drop into boiling salted water and cook for 18 minutes or until just tender. Drain in a colander and run fresh cold water through them for a few seconds. This will help them to skin easily. (Canned potatoes need draining and drying only.) Heat the butter in a large frying pan and when foaming put in the potatoes and fry gently, stirring frequently until golden brown and slightly crisp. Serve sprinkled with salt and herbs.

700 g (1½ lb) small new potatoes (fresh or canned)
salt
50 g (2 oz) butter
1 tablespoon chopped parsley
1 tablespoon chopped chives or spring onion tops

Serves 4

Gratin Dauphinois
Potatoes Baked with Cream

1 kg (2 lb) potatoes
1 clove garlic (optional)
50 g (2 oz) butter
salt and ground black pepper
about 250 ml (½ pint) milk
125 ml (¼ pint) double cream

Serves 6

Peel the potatoes and cut into thin slices about the thickness of a 10p piece (a mandoline cutter will do this job very efficiently). Peel and crush the garlic, if used, and mix with the butter. Use about one-third of the butter to grease a shallow baking dish generously. Arrange the potatoes in the dish in layers, sprinkling each layer with salt and pepper. Pour over enough milk just to cover the potatoes, and dot with the remaining butter. Cook in a slow oven 150°C, 300°F or Gas Mark 2 until the potatoes are tender and most of the milk absorbed (about 1 hour). Pour the cream over the potatoes, and continue cooking for a further half hour, until the potatoes are creamy and the surface golden.

Cocktail de Champignons
Mushroom Cocktail

200 g (8 oz) bacon *or* ham
75 g (3 oz) butter
450 g (1 lb) button mushrooms
2 tablespoons oil
1 small clove garlic, peeled
chopped parsley
12 small green olives, stoned
ground black pepper
salt if necessary

Serves 4

Discard any rinds or bones from the bacon or ham and cut the meat into 5 mm (¼-inch) dice. Heat 25 g (1 oz) of the butter in a small pan, add the bacon or ham and sauté until just beginning to colour, about 5 minutes. Wash the mushrooms, but do not peel them. Heat the oil and remaining butter in a large frying pan, add the mushrooms and fry fairly briskly until they have given out all their liquid. Chop the garlic finely and add to the mushrooms with the parsley. Stir and fry for another minute or two, then add the olives, seasoning to taste, and the ham or bacon. Serve very hot.

This cocktail goes very well with roast pork, veal, or beef. It is also good by itself as a first course, garnished with sippets of crisply fried bread.

Petits Pois à la Paysanne
Country Style Green Peas

10 spring onions *or* button onions
10–12 large outside leaves of lettuce
50 g (2 oz) butter
450 g (1 lb) shelled green peas, fresh
  or frozen
1 bay leaf
1 small sprig thyme
2 tablespoons water
salt and ground black pepper

Serves 4 or 5

Peel the onions and remove the green part if using spring onions. Wash the lettuce leaves. Melt the butter in a flame-proof casserole and fry the onions over low heat for a few minutes. Add the lettuce leaves, then cover, and cook slowly for 5 minutes, or until the lettuce begins to wilt. Add the peas, bay leaf, thyme, water and seasoning. Cover tightly and cook very gently for about 40–50 minutes, until the peas are tender. This can be done over a very low heat on top of the cooker, using an asbestos mat if necessary, or in the lower part of a moderate oven. To serve, check the seasoning, remove the herbs, and turn all the rest into a hot vegetable dish.

Salsifis Frits
Salsify Fritters

Wash the salsify roots, peel them one by one and cut into pieces roughly the size of a little finger. As each one is ready, drop immediately into acidulated cold water (1 tablespoon vinegar per 500 ml (1 pint) of water). When they are all ready, drain them, then drop into boiling salted water and cook until almost tender, from 20–30 minutes depending on the age of the salsify. Do not overcook. Drain and dry the pieces. When ready to fry, heat a deep pan of oil to frying temperature 190°C, 375°F. Dip the pieces of salsify one by one into the batter, then lower into the hot fat. As soon as the batter is golden and crisp, remove the fritters and drain on absorbent paper. Serve immediately with quarters of lemon.

These salsify fritters are not only excellent as an accompaniment for any roast meat or as a vegetable dish on their own, but are a delicious and unusual cocktail savoury.

450 g (1 lb) salsify *or* scorzonera
vinegar
salt
oil for deep frying
Frying Batter (p. 30)
1 lemon, quartered

Serves 4

Timbale d'Epinards
Spinach Timbale

Strictly speaking, a timbale should be unmoulded and served surrounded by sauce. To do this, generously butter a 1 litre (2 pint) soufflé dish or mould and coat evenly with breadcrumbs. If, however, you serve it in the dish the browned crumbs can be omitted.

Preheat a moderately hot oven 190°C, 375°F or Gas Mark 5. Wash the spinach thoroughly and remove any tough stalks. Put into a large saucepan without additional water, and cook, covered, for about 10 minutes or until tender. Drain thoroughly, and when cool enough to handle squeeze as dry as possible, then pass through the coarse mesh of a vegetable mill, or chop very finely. Soak the bread in a little milk, then squeeze dry. Cream the 25 g (1 oz) butter in a large basin. Stir in the breadcrumbs, the egg yolks one by one, the nutmeg, sugar, salt and pepper, and finally the spinach. Whip the egg whites until stiff and fold lightly but thoroughly into the mixture. Turn into the mould and bake in the centre of the oven for 25–30 minutes, until just firm in the centre. Serve with the hot Tomato Sauce.

700 g (1½ lb) fresh spinach
1 slice white crustless bread (25 g or 1 oz)
a little milk
25 g (1 oz) butter
2 eggs, separated
grating of nutmeg
pinch sugar
salt and ground black pepper
butter for greasing the mould
browned breadcrumbs for coating (optional)
250 ml (½ pint) Tomato Sauce (p. 40) to accompany

Serves 3 or 4

Couronne Végétarienne
Spinach and Cauliflower Crown

1 kg (2 lb) fresh spinach
salt
1 small cauliflower
butter for greasing the mould
250 ml (½ pint) pouring Béchamel
    Sauce (p. 33)
a little tomato purée *or* paprika

Serves 4

Wash the spinach thoroughly and discard any tough stalks. Pack it into a large saucepan without additional water, add 1 teaspoon of salt, and cook over moderate heat for 10–15 minutes, until tender, stirring occasionally. (If using tough winter spinach have 2 tablespoons boiling water in the bottom of the pan before adding the spinach.) Trim the cauliflower of leaves and stalk, and wash. Cook whole, in boiling salted water for 10–15 minutes until *just* tender. Drain it, taking care to keep it whole. Drain the spinach thoroughly, squeeze as dry as possible, then chop roughly. Well butter a 16–18 cm (6–7 inch) ring mould, and pack the spinach into it firmly. Unmould it carefully into a fairly wide deep dish and arrange the cauliflower in the middle of the ring. Colour the Béchamel Sauce pink with the tomato purée or paprika, check the seasoning, and reheat. Pour the sauce round the outside of the spinach ring, and serve immediately.

Fenouil Gratiné
Fennel au Gratin

4 bulbs of Florentine fennel
salt
40 g (1½ oz) butter
ground black pepper
50 g (2 oz) grated Parmesan cheese

Serves 4

Trim the fennel roots if necessary and wipe with a damp cloth. Cut in half lengthways. Drop into boiling salted water and simmer, covered, for 25–30 minutes or until tender. Drain thoroughly. Arrange rounded side up in a single layer in a generously buttered ovenproof dish. Sprinkle lightly with salt and pepper and thickly with cheese. Dot with the remaining butter and brown lightly under a preheated grill. Serve hot with lamb or pork chops, or with chicken.

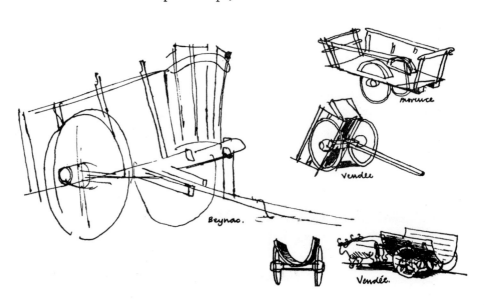

Topinambours au Jus
Braised Jerusalem Artichokes

Peel the artichokes and immediately drop into acidulated cold water (1 tablespoon lemon juice per 500 ml (1 pint) water). When ready to cook, drain and dry them and cut into slices about the thickness of a 10p coin. Melt 50 g (2 oz) of the butter in a wide saucepan, put in the artichokes and cook gently, stirring frequently, for 10 minutes. Sprinkle with salt and pepper, add the stock or jus de viande, and cook gently, covered, until almost tender. Remove the lid and continue cooking until most of the liquid has evaporated. Add the remaining butter, a squeeze of lemon juice and the parsley, and shake the pan to distribute them evenly.

700 g (1½ lb) Jerusalem artichokes
lemon juice
65 g (2½ oz) unsalted butter
salt and ground black pepper
5 tablespoons concentrated chicken stock *or* jus de viande (p. 23)
juice of ½ lemon
a little finely chopped parsley

Serves 4

Tomates à la Provencale
Stuffed Tomatoes

Cut the tomatoes horizontally in half, and with the back of a spoon make a depression in the centre. Sprinkle generously with salt and pepper. Crush the clove of garlic with ¼ teaspoon salt, mix with the parsley and breadcrumbs, and add sufficient oil to moisten thoroughly. Divide this mixture between the tomatoes, pressing it well into the depression. Arrange them side by side in an oiled ovenproof dish. Cook them under a gentle grill until the tomatoes are tender, then increase the heat to brown the surface. Alternatively, if you are using the oven, cook them in a moderately hot oven preheated to 190°C, 375°F or Gas Mark 5 for 15–20 minutes, or rather longer in a cooler oven.

Excellent with roast or grilled chicken, lamb or white fish.

6 large firm tomatoes
salt and ground black pepper
2 cloves garlic, peeled
2 tablespoons chopped parsley
40 g (1½ oz) dry white breadcrumbs
about 6 tablespoons olive oil

Serves 6

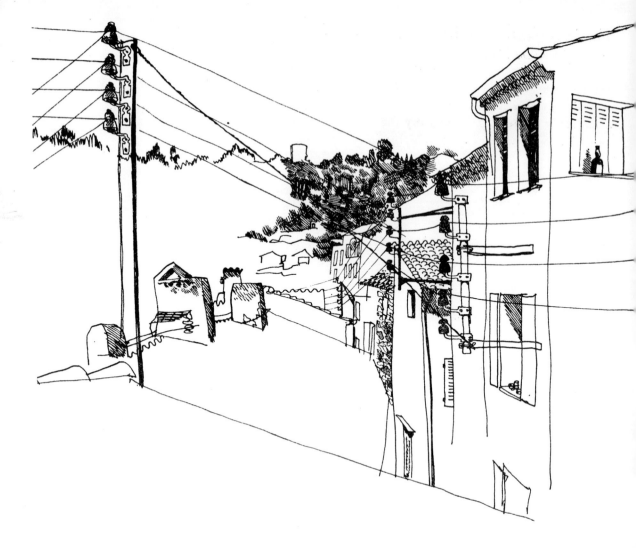

Haricots Verts à la Maître d'Hôtel
French Beans Maître d'Hôtel

1 kg (2 lb) young French beans
salt and ground black pepper
50 g (2 oz) butter
2 teaspoons lemon juice
1 tablespoon chopped parsley

Serves 4–6

Top and tail the beans which should be much too young to require stringing. Prepare a large pan of fast boiling salted water, and add the beans a handful at a time. Bring the water back to the boil rapidly, then boil gently, uncovered, for 10–12 minutes or until *just* tender. Drain immediately. Return to the pan and toss over moderate heat for a minute or so, then add salt, freshly ground pepper and the butter. Toss to distribute evenly, then add the lemon juice and parsley and turn into a hot vegetable dish. Serve immediately.

Note If it is not possible to serve immediately, complete the preliminary cooking then drain and cool rapidly under cold running water. Drain again and keep cool. When required, reheat by tossing in the butter over moderate heat for several minutes.

Les Poissons, Coquillages et Crustacés

Fish, Shellfish and Crustacea

Around the coasts of France, and often inland as well, it is a revelation to visit a fish shop or market stall. The variety of unusual species, vibrant colours, and obvious freshness are enough to overcome any qualms one might have about tackling the unknown. However, Francine must have confined her fish shopping to Paris because most of her recipes are for species which, more often than not, can be found in the average fish shop. The delicate texture and flavour of fish should never be subjected to the rough treatment of boiling and you will note that many of Francine's recipes are first poached in a herb and wine flavoured stock or 'court bouillon'.

The various cold fish dishes make a welcome change in hot weather, or they can provide original meal starters at any time of the year.

Bar à la Dumas
Cold Bass with Dumas Sauce

Ask the fishmonger to gut and scale the fish. Put into the court bouillon, bring slowly to the boil then poach for 25–30 minutes. Leave to cool in the court bouillon, then drain, and slide on to a serving dish.

Cut the hard-boiled eggs in half lengthways. Remove the yolks, mash them and mix into half of the mayonnaise, with the gherkins and herbs. Fill six of the egg whites with this mixture. Fill the remaining six whites with some of the Dumas Sauce.

Arrange the stuffed eggs alternately round the fish. Garnish the mayonnaise-stuffed eggs with the green olives, and the eggs stuffed with Dumas Sauce with the black olives.

Serve the remaining mayonnaise and Dumas Sauce in separate bowls.

1 bass, about 1½ kg (3 lb)
cold Court Bouillon (p. 28)
6 hard-boiled eggs
250 ml (½ pint) stiff mayonnaise
2 gherkins, finely chopped
1 tablespoon chopped mixed parsley, chervil, chives and tarragon
250 ml (½ pint) Dumas Sauce (p. 35)
6 green olives
6 black olives

Serves 6

Langouste Francette
Crawfish (or Lobster) Francette

Ask the fishmonger to split the crawfish or lobster in half lengthways and remove the head. Take out the tail meat and cut it, on the slant, into equal sized slices. Chop the claw meat fairly finely. Reserve the shells.

Cut the mushrooms into thin slices. Heat half of the butter in a sauté pan and fry the mushrooms gently until they have given off all their liquid. Melt the remaining butter in a heavy saucepan, add the flour and cook, stirring, for 2 minutes, then little by little, stir in the fish stock smoothly and simmer gently, stirring, until thickened. Cut a few slices of truffle and reserve for garnishing; chop the rest and add to the sauce with the truffle liquid. Add the mushrooms and their butter; and, if the sauce is too thick, add a little more stock—it should be fairly runny as the egg and cream still have to be added. Season with cayenne, salt and pepper. Put the slices of crawfish into the sauce, stir and heat through, then remove them and keep hot. Stir in the chopped claw meat and simmer for a few minutes. Take off the heat and stir in the egg yolk and cream. Fill the shells with the sauce, arrange the slices of crawfish on top and garnish with the reserved pieces of truffle.

Plain boiled rice goes well with this dish.

1 cooked crawfish *or* lobster, about 1–1¼ kg (2–2½ lb)
450 g (1 lb) firm mushrooms, washed
75 g (3 oz) butter
2 level tablespoons flour
250 ml (½ pint) Fish Stock (p. 28)
15 g (½ oz) can truffles (optional)
pinch cayenne
salt and ground black pepper
1 egg yolk, well beaten
2 tablespoons double cream

Serves 4

Anguilles aux Herbes
Eel with Herbs

1 kg (2 lb) eel
1 lettuce
1 handful sorrel *or* spinach
½ handful parsley
1 tablespoon mixed fresh chervil,
    sage and tarragon
30 g (generous 1 oz) butter
large pinch powdered dried thyme
large pinch powdered bay leaf
250 ml (½ pint) dry white wine
salt and ground black pepper
2 small egg yolks
squeeze of lemon juice

Serves 4

Have the eel cut into 5 cm (2 inch) pieces. Wash the vegetables and fresh herbs, discard tough stalks, shake dry, and chop all very finely. Melt the butter in a heavy pan and sauté the chopped vegetables and herbs quickly for a minute or two. Add the eel, dried thyme and bay leaf, wine, salt and pepper. Bring quickly to the boil then cover the pan and simmer gently for 25–30 minutes, stirring occasionally. Beat the egg yolks in a basin. Strain a little of the stock from the eel saucepan and add, little by little, to the egg yolks, whisking all the time. Return all to the eels, stirring over gentle heat until the sauce thickens slightly; do not allow to boil. Take off the heat, squeeze in the lemon juice, and check the seasoning.

    Serve the eel, vegetables and sauce together in a deep dish. This can be eaten hot or cold.

Mulet au Citron
Grey Mullet with Lemon

1 grey mullet about 1–1¼ kg (2–2½ lb)
1 lemon
1 sweet pepper
3 tomatoes, peeled
1 small stick celery, washed
2 cloves garlic, peeled
3 shallots, peeled
1 heaped tablespoon parsley sprigs
4 tablespoons olive oil
1 sprig thyme
1 small bay leaf
1 level teaspoon paprika
pinch mixed spice
salt and ground black pepper

Serves 4 or 5

Ask the fishmonger to clean and scale the mullet, but to leave the head on.

    Cut the lemon into thin slices and cut each slice in half. Place the mullet flat in a shallow ovenproof dish. With a sharp knife, make deep incisions across the width of the fish, spaced at 2½ cm (1 inch) intervals down the length of the fish. Press a half slice of lemon into each cut.

    Halve the pepper and remove the core and seeds. Chop the pepper, tomatoes, celery, garlic, shallots and parsley together finely. Put into a basin, add all the remaining ingredients and mix well. Spoon this mixture round the fish, and bake in a moderate oven preheated to 190°C, 375°F or Gas Mark 5 for 30–40 minutes, basting frequently. Remove the thyme and bay leaf and serve in the same dish.

Poisson Grillé au Fenouil
Grilled Fish with Fennel

suitable whole fish, weight 1–1¼ kg
    (2–2½ lb)*
salt and ground black pepper
olive oil
dried fennel stalks
2 tablespoons brandy
some lemon slices
fennel foliage to garnish, if available
Rémoulade Sauce (p. 38) (optional)

Serves 4 or 5
*a firm fleshed fish such as red *or*
    grey mullet *or* sea bass

Clean the fish and scale if necessary. Make several incisions on each side with a sharp knife, season, and brush with olive oil. Preheat a medium grill, then grill the fish for 5–8 minutes on each side, depending on thickness. Spread a thick layer of fennel stalks on a *flameproof* dish, and over it stand a metal grid. Lay the partially cooked fish on the grid. Heat the brandy, set it alight and pour flaming over the fish, when it should, in turn, set light to the fennel twigs. Allow the fish to cook for a few more minutes on each side, then transfer it carefully to a serving dish. Garnish with slices of lemon and, if available, some feathery fennel foliage.

Serve with or without Rémoulade Sauce.

L'Aiglefin au Concombre
Cold Haddock with Cucumber

Put the haddock into the court bouillon and bring slowly to the boil. Simmer gently for 25–30 minutes. Drain the fish and leave to become cold.

Peel and finely slice the cucumber, put it in a colander, sprinkle with salt and leave for at least half an hour.

Remove all skin and bones from the fish, flake the fish coarsely and sprinkle with the lemon juice. Arrange down the middle of a large serving dish and dust with paprika.

Season the cream with pepper, fold in the drained cucumber slices and the parsley, and spoon it round the fish. Keep very cold and, just before serving, sprinkle a few drops of vinegar over the fish.

1 whole fresh haddock, about 1½ kg (3 lb)
cold Court Bouillon (p. 28)
1 medium cucumber
salt and white pepper
juice of 1 lemon
a little paprika pepper
125 ml (¼ pint) double cream
1 tablespoon chopped parsley
a little shallot flavoured vinegar

Serves 6

Tranches de Flétan à la Mornay
Halibut Steaks Mornay

Trim the halibut steaks if necessary. Generously butter an ovenproof dish, put in the steaks, sprinkle with salt and pepper, and cover with a well buttered piece of kitchen foil. Cook in a moderate oven preheated to 190°C, 375°F or Gas Mark 5 for 25–30 minutes. When the fish is cooked, drain any cooking liquid into the Mornay Sauce and whisk over heat until reduced to a light coating consistency. Pour over the fish, and sprinkle evenly with the cheese. Put back into a hot oven 220°C, 425°F or Gas Mark 7 for 10 minutes, or until the sauce is bubbling and the cheese golden.

Cod, hake or fresh haddock can be cooked in the same way, but a simple Mornay Sauce (p. 34) should then be used.

4 halibut steaks, about 150 g (6 oz) each
butter for greasing
salt and white pepper
rich Mornay Sauce (p. 34)
50 g (2 oz) grated Parmesan *or* Gruyère cheese

Serves 4

Flétan à la Basquaise
Halibut Steaks Basque Style

Heat 2 tablespoons of the oil in a wide flameproof casserole and fry the fish in the oil until lightly browned on both sides. Season with salt and pepper, cover the casserole, and cook in a moderate oven preheated to 180°C, 350°F or Gas Mark 4 for 20 minutes. Meanwhile, thinly slice the onions, and peel, de-seed and chop the tomatoes. Remove the fish from the casserole

4 tablespoons olive oil
2 thick slices halibut, about 350 g (generous 12 oz) each
salt and ground black pepper
300 g (12 oz) onions, peeled
300 g (12 oz) tomatoes

Serves 4

83

and keep warm. If necessary, add another tablespoon of oil to the casserole, heat on top of the cooker and fry the onions gently for 10 minutes or until soft and golden. Add the tomatoes and cook, stirring now and then, for about 5 minutes, until the excess moisture has been driven off. Replace the fish, spoon some of the onion and tomato mixture over it, cover, and allow to heat very gently on top of the cooker, or in the oven, for 5–10 minutes. Serve the fish with the contents of the casserole poured over it.

This recipe can also be used for slices of fresh tuna fish, allowing a longer cooking time.

Gratin d'Homard
Blazed Lobster au Gratin

1 large cooked lobster, about 2¼ kg
  (4½ lb)
2 shallots, peeled
100 g (½ oz) butter
40 g (14 oz) flour
375 ml (¾ pint) Court Bouillon (p. 28)
1 level tablespoon tomato purée
salt and ground black pepper
125 ml (¼ pint) double cream
15 g (½ oz) can truffles (optional)
3 tablespoons brandy

Serves 5

Ask the fishmonger to split the lobster in half lengthways. Remove the tail meat and cut across in equal slices. Take out all the rest of the meat and chop it.

Finely chop the shallots. Melt 50 g (2 oz) of the butter in a saucepan and gently fry the shallots for 5 minutes until soft. Add the *slices* of lobster and cook *gently* until lightly coloured on both sides. Melt remaining butter in another saucepan, add the flour and cook, stirring for 2 minutes. Little by little stir in the court bouillon, followed by the tomato purée, salt and pepper; stir until boiling, then simmer for two minutes. Add the chopped lobster and cream to the sauce.

Turn the lobster slices and shallots into a gratin dish, cover with the sauce, and set under a hot grill until the sauce begins to bubble and brown.

Slice the truffles, if used. Immediately before serving, heat the brandy, light it and pour flaming over the lobster. When the flame has gone out, garnish with the truffle slices, if used, and serve at once.

Coquilles d'Homard
Cold Lobster in Scallop Shells

1 lettuce
250 ml (½ pint) Mayonnaise (p. 37)
1 cooked lobster, about 650 g (1½ lb)
1 tablespoon chopped mixed parsley
  and chervil
3 hard-boiled eggs
6 anchovy fillets (optional)
6 stuffed olives (optional)

Serves 6

For this dish you will need six deep scallop shells or individual dishes. Wash the lettuce, dry the leaves, and then shred them finely and mix with a little of the mayonnaise. Divide among the shells, making a bed for the other ingredients. Chop all the meat from the lobster claws, and arrange on the lettuce. Coat with mayonnaise and sprinkle with the herbs. Slice the meat from the lobster tail and arrange on top of the mayonnaise. Quarter the hard-boiled eggs lengthways, and arrange two pieces on each of the shells with a curled anchovy fillet and stuffed olive between.

Maquereaux Marmande
Mackerel with Mushrooms and Onions

Ask the fishmonger to head, split and bone the mackerel.

Chop the tomatoes roughly, and sauté gently in 1 tablespoon of the oil for about 5 minutes, or until most of their liquid has evaporated. Season and keep hot. Meanwhile, finely chop the mushrooms, onion, shallots and garlic, mix together, and then sauté gently in 2 tablespoons of the oil until the onion is soft; season and keep hot.

Season about 2 tablespoons of flour with salt and pepper and coat the mackerel with it, pressing the coating on firmly. Heat about 3 tablespoons of oil in a large frying pan, and when hot fry the mackerel for 3–4 minutes each side, until cooked through and golden. Drain carefully, and arrange on a hot serving dish. Spoon the mushroom and onion mixture over the mackerel, surround with the tomatoes, and dust with the herbs.

4 fresh mackerel
450 g (1 lb) tomatoes, peeled
about 6 tablespoons olive oil
salt and ground black pepper
200 g (8 oz) mushrooms, washed
1 large onion, peeled
2 shallots, peeled
1 clove garlic, peeled
a little seasoned flour
1 heaped tablespoon chopped mixed
    parsley, chervil, chives and
    tarragon

Serves 4

Rougets à la Bordelaise
Red Mullet with Bordelaise Sauce

Ask the fishmonger to gut and scale the fish but leave the heads on. Arrange them side by side in an ovenproof dish, season with salt and pepper, and pour the butter over them. Cook in a moderate oven preheated to 190°C, 375°F or Gas Mark 5 for 25–30 minutes, basting frequently. Serve the sauce separately.

6 small red mullet, about 200 g (8 oz)
    each
salt and ground black pepper
50 g (2 oz) melted butter
Bordelaise Sauce (p. 35)

Serves 6

Moules à la Crème
Cold Mussels in Cream Sauce

Scrape and clean the mussels in several changes of cold water, discarding any that do not shut tightly. Put them into a large saucepan with the shallots, garlic, thyme, bay leaf, spice, saffron and salt and pepper. Pour in the wine, bring to the boil, and boil briskly for 5 or 6 minutes, until the mussels have opened. Shake the pan during the cooking so that they cook evenly. Remove the mussels with a perforated spoon, and when cool take them out of their shells and put into a serving bowl. Strain the mussel stock through several folds of muslin to remove all traces of sand, then return to the rinsed saucepan and heat. Whisk the egg yolks in a bowl and, little by little, whisk in the stock. Return to the saucepan and stir over *very low* heat until the sauce thickens enough to coat the back of a wooden spoon; do not let it boil. Pour the cream into a bowl, and little by little whisk the sauce into the cream. Taste and adjust the seasoning, then pour over the mussels, and keep very cold until they are served.

3½ litres (6 pints) fresh mussels
3 shallots, peeled and chopped
1 clove garlic, peeled
1 sprig thyme
1 bay leaf
pinch mixed spice
pinch saffron
salt and ground black pepper
500 ml (1 pint) good dry white wine
3 egg yolks
125 ml (¼ pint) double cream

Serves 6

Quenelles de Brochet
Pike Quenelles

550 g (1½ lb) boned, skinned pike
salt and white pepper
250 ml (½ pint) water
50 g (2 oz) butter
100 g (4 oz) sifted flour
2 eggs
2 egg whites
4–6 tablespoons double cream
Nantua Sauce (p. 39)

Serves 6–8

Pass the raw fish twice through the mincer, then season with salt and pepper. Put the water, butter and a level teaspoon of salt into a medium sized saucepan and bring to the boil. As soon as the butter has melted, add the flour all at once and beat with a wooden spoon over moderate heat until the mixture forms a ball and leaves the sides of the pan. Remove from the heat. Beat the eggs and egg whites together lightly, then beat into the mixture little by little, making sure the last addition is absorbed before adding the next. Finally beat in the fish, mixing thoroughly. Chill in the refrigerator for 2 hours. Chill the cream at the same time.

When ready to cook fill a wide pan with water to a depth of about 7½ cm (3 inches) and bring to simmering point.

With a wooden spoon beat the cream, spoonful by spoonful, into the fish mixture, beating very thoroughly and stopping if the mixture shows signs of becoming too soft. Using two dessert spoons dipped in cold water, shape the mixture into egg shapes and slide into the barely simmering water as they are prepared. Poach them, uncovered, for 15–20 minutes. When cooked they will have increased in size and roll over readily. Remove them with a perforated spoon, arrange them in a serving dish and keep warm.

Heat the Nantua Sauce and serve the quenelles with the sauce poured over them.

Editor's note Brill, halibut or coley are also suitable for quenelles.

Filets de Sole Aurore
Fillets of Sole with Cream Sauce

6 sole, about 200–300 g (8–12 oz) each
Fish Stock (p. 28)
250 ml (½ pint) very thick Béchamel Sauce p. (33)
juice of 1 lemon
about 2 tablespoons concentrated tomato purée
2 egg yolks
4 tablespoons double cream
salt and ground black pepper

Serves 6

Ask the fishmonger to skin and fillet the sole and to give you the heads, bones and skins. Use these to make the stock.

Strain the stock into a wide saucepan and gently poach the fillets of sole in it for about 10 minutes. Lift out and drain carefully, then arrange the fillets in a serving dish and keep hot.

Heat the Béchamel Sauce gently, and whisk in, little by little, enough of the fish stock to thin the sauce to a coating consistency. Add the lemon juice, and then sufficient tomato purée to colour the sauce well. Bring to the boil then remove the pan from the heat. Whisk the egg yolks and cream together and whisk into the sauce. Check the seasoning and pour the sauce over the fillets.

These fillets can be garnished with cooked mussels or sliced crawfish tails.

Filets de Sole Normande
Fillets of Sole Normandy

Ask the fishmonger to skin and fillet the sole and give you the heads, bones and skins.

Wash and scrub the mussels in several changes of cold water, discarding any that do not shut tightly. Put the mussels into a saucepan with the sole debris and wine, and cook over brisk heat for 5–6 minutes or until the mussels open. As soon as they open, take out the mussels and discard their shells. Strain and reserve the stock.

Heat the butter and sauté the mushrooms very gently for 10 minutes.

Put the mussel stock into a wide shallow pan and, when simmering, put in the fish fillets, season them and poach for 5–7 minutes. When cooked, drain, arrange on a serving dish and keep warm, reserving the stock.

Stir the mushrooms and their juices into the Béchamel Sauce, add the shrimps, and then stir in enough stock to make a light coating consistency. Stir over gentle heat until hot, adjust the seasoning and pour the sauce over the fish. Serve immediately.

3 sole, about 450 g (1 lb) each
1 litre (scant 2 pints) fresh mussels
250 ml (½ pint) dry white wine
30 g (generous 1 oz) butter
200 g (8 oz) button mushrooms, washed
salt and ground black pepper
500 ml (1 pint) coating Béchamel Sauce (p. 33)
100 g)4 oz) peeled shrimps

Serves 6

Sole Forestière
Sole Baked with Mushrooms and Shallots

Ask the fishmonger to remove the heads and dark skin, and to trim the sole.

Slice the mushrooms and sauté gently in half of the butter until all their liquid has evaporated. Lay the sole in a large ovenproof dish, if possible without overlapping. Finely chop the shallots and parsley, mix them, and sprinkle evenly over the sole. Dot with the remaining butter and surround with the mushrooms. Pour in the wine and add seasoning to taste. Cook in a moderate oven preheated to 190°C, 375°F or Gas Mark 5 for 15–20 minutes, basting frequently. Sprinkle with lemon juice just before serving.

4 Dover *or* lemon sole, about 200–300 g (8–12 oz) each
200 g (8 oz) firm mushrooms, washed
75 g (3 oz) butter
3 shallots, peeled
1 heaped tablespoon chopped parsley
125 ml (¼ pint) dry white wine
salt and ground black pepper
juice of ½ lemon

Serves 4

Filets de Sole Tante Marie
Fillets of Sole Tante Marie

Ask the fishmonger to clean the fish and remove the dark skin and the heads.

Chop the mushrooms very finely, then simmer them for 10–15 minutes with 50 g (2 oz) of the butter, 6 tablespoons of the cream, and salt and pepper, until they are a purée. Finely chop the shallots. Butter a large ovenproof dish, arrange the sole in it, add the wine, stock, shallots, salt and pepper and bake in

6 sole, about 200–300 g (8–12 oz) each
200 g (8 oz) firm mushrooms, washed
75 g (3 oz) butter
8 tablespoons double cream
salt and ground black pepper
125 ml (¼ pint) white wine
6 shallots, peeled
125 ml (¼ pint) jellied stock (p. 27)
15 g (½ oz) can truffles (optional)
Croûtons to garnish (p. 21)

Serves 6

a moderate oven preheated to 190°C, 375°F or Gas Mark 5 for 15 minutes, basting occasionally. Remove the sole to a chopping board, reserving their stock. Lift the whole of one side of each fish carefully off the backbone and take out all the bones. If there are any roes, mash them and add to the mushroom purée with the remaining cream. Spread some of this stuffing on each sole then cover with the other half of the fish. Arrange side by side in an ovenproof dish. Add the remaining butter to the fish stock, boil rapidly, uncovered, to reduce it to about 125 ml (¼-pint) then strain it over the fish. Return to the oven for about 10 minutes. Serve the fish garnished with slices of truffle, if used, and the croûtons.

Filets de Sole au Vermouth
Fillets of Sole with Vermouth

4 Dover *or* lemon sole, about 200–300 g (8–12 oz) each
250 ml (½ pint) Fish Stock (p. 28)
125 ml (¼ pint) French vermouth
salt and white pepper
50 g (2 oz) butter
2 egg yolks
1 tablespoon double cream

Serves 4

Have the sole skinned and filleted and ask the fishmonger for the heads, bones and skins. Use these to make the stock (p. 28), beginning with 500 ml (1 pint) of water and reducing by fast boiling to 250 ml (½-pint). Add the vermouth to the strained stock, taste, and adjust the seasoning. Roll the fillets with the skin side inside. Butter a large ovenproof gratin dish, arrange the rolled fillets side by side and pour the stock and vermouth over them. Cover with a piece of buttered greaseproof paper and poach in a moderate oven preheated to 180°C, 350°F or Gas Mark 4 for 15 minutes. Strain the stock into a small saucepan and boil fast, uncovered, to reduce it by about one-third. Whisk it little by little into the egg yolks, then add the cream. Return to the saucepan and whisk over low heat, adding the remaining butter in small pieces, until the sauce begins to thicken; but do not let it boil. Pour over the fish and serve immediately.

Langoustines à la Martine
Scampi Martine

Roughly chop the ham, carrots, onion and shallots. Melt the butter in a saucepan, add the chopped ingredients, the bacon bone and either the garlic or parsley. Fry for 5 minutes or until lightly coloured, stirring frequently. Stir in the flour, a few grinds of black pepper and the wine, and bring to the boil. Cover the pan tightly and simmer very gently for 1½ hours (or reduce the quantity of wine to 375 ml (¾-pint) and pressure cook for 20 minutes). When the ham and vegetable mixture is nearly ready, cook the rice in plenty of boiling salted water until *just* tender, then drain, dry and keep warm.

Remove the bacon bone and purée the ham and vegetable mixture in an electric blender or pass through a vegetable mill. Return the purée to the saucepan, add the scampi (previously sliced if they are large ones) and heat gently for 5 minutes. Check the seasoning.

Form the rice into a ring on a hot dish and serve the scampi mixture in the centre.

100 g (4 oz) cooked ham
250 g (10 oz) young carrots, peeled
1 large onion, peeled
2 shallots, peeled
50 g (2 oz) butter
1 bacon bone
1 clove garlic, peeled *or* 4 sprigs parsley
1 level tablespoon flour
ground black pepper
500 ml (1 pint) white wine
200 g (8 oz) long grain rice
450 g (1 lb) peeled scampi

Serves 3 or 4

Truites aux Amandes
Trout with Almonds

Ask the fishmonger to clean the trout through the gills but to leave the heads on.

Dry the fish and then roll in seasoned flour, pressing the flour on firmly. Melt 50 g (2 oz) of the butter in a large frying pan and, when hot, put in the trout and fry gently for 4–5 minutes each side, until cooked and golden. Transfer carefully to a serving dish and keep hot in the oven. Add the remaining butter to the frying pan, and when hot add the almonds and fry, stirring frequently, until even browned. Add the wine, heat for a minute and then pour almonds and wine over the trout.

4 fresh trout, about 150 g (6 oz) each
a little seasoned flour
75 g (3 oz) unsalted butter
100 g (4 oz) flaked almonds
6 tablespoons dry white wine

Serves 4

Turbot Poché, Sauce Mousseline
Poached Turbot with Mousseline Sauce

Arrange the slices of turbot in a single layer in a wide pan. Pour the court bouillon over them and bring slowly to simmering point. Cover the pan and simmer gently for 10–12 minutes. Meanwhile, make the sauce. Drain the fish carefully and remove any dark skin.

Arrange the fish on a serving dish, garnish with the lemon and parsley, and serve the sauce separately.

4 slices turbot, about 150–200 g (6–8 oz) each
cold Court Bouillon (p. 28), half quantity
Mousseline Sauce (p. 28)
4 thin slices lemon
4 sprigs fresh parsley

Serves 4

Filets de Poissons à la Bretonne
Fish Fillets Brittany Style

6 fillets of white fish, about 150 g
  (6 oz) each
some seasoned flour
100 g (4 oz) butter
2 tablespoons oil
1 heaped tablespoon finely chopped
  shallot
100 g (4 oz) shelled shrimps *or*
  prawns
1 rounded tablespoon capers
1 rounded tablespoon chopped mixed
  parsley, chives and chervil
juice of 1 large lemon

Serves 6

Coat the fillets evenly with seasoned flour and press the coating on firmly. Heat 40 g (1½ oz) of the butter and 1 tablespoon of the oil in a frying pan and fry half of the fillets, skin side uppermost first, for 3–6 minutes each side, depending on thickness. Drain carefully, arrange on a serving dish and keep hot while the remaining fillets are fried in another 40 g (1½ oz) of butter and the rest of the oil. Meanwhile, melt the remaining butter in a small frying pan and fry the shallot *gently* until soft. Add the shrimps or prawns, capers, herbs and lemon juice, heat gently and then pour over the fish.

Raie au Beurre Noir et Câpres
Skate with Browned Butter Capers

Court Bouillon (p. 28)
4 portions of skate wing, about 200 g
  (8 oz) each
50 g (2 oz) butter
2 tablespoons wine vinegar
1 heaped tablespoon drained capers
1 level tablespoon chopped parsley

Serves 4

Heat the court bouillon in a wide saucepan, and when simmering add the pieces of skate. Simmer gently for 12–15 minutes. Drain the fish, cut off the outer thin boney fringe, and arrange the fish on a very hot serving dish.

Heat the butter in a small frying pan until it turns nut brown then pour at once over the fish. Heat the wine vinegar in the same pan, let it bubble for a minute or two, then add the capers and pour over the fish. Sprinkle with parsley and serve immediately.

La Volaille et le Gibier

Poultry and Game

The poultry that Francine bought and cooked in Paris before the Second World War would have been free range, suitably hung, and drawn and plucked shortly before cooking. Apart from the obvious differences this would have made to their texture and flavour, her recipes adapt easily to our less substantial, less tasty, mass-produced poultry. Francine uses butter, herbs, wine and vegetables generously, and if not strictly classical, her recipes are full of colour and flavour. The cream that features in so many recipes would, of course, be well matured thick cream to add the richness that young chicken lack.

The pigeon recipes do much to raise the status of this humble bird but, when buying, be sure to look for young plump and tender specimens such as the French raise specially for the table.

The success of cooked game depends very largely on the condition of the game before cooking. This in turn depends upon the knowledge and judgement used in the handling and preparation of the game during the time between killing and actually cooking. The uninitiated would be wise to rely on the services of traditional game merchants, most of whom are happy to advise as well as to supply merchandise. When ordering game remember to say whether you like it well hung and tasty, or whether you prefer a fresher flavour.

Some of Francine's recipes are suitable for young game, others for older casserole birds. The recipes have been edited to include this information, and also to give relevant notes about average sizes, seasons and peak condition times.

Poulet à la Basquaise
Chicken in Basque Style

Cut the chicken into six joints. Heat 50 g (2 oz) of the butter and the oil in a heavy saucepan and brown the joints, turning them frequently. Cover the pan, and cook over very low heat (use an asbestos or wire mat if necessary) for 45 minutes. Meanwhile, melt the remaining butter in a heavy saucepan, put in the tomatoes, sprinkle with salt and pepper, cover, and cook over very low heat until the tomatoes are soft but not breaking up (about 20 minutes). When the chicken is done, remove the joints from the pan, arrange on a serving dish and keep hot. Pour the wine, brandy and stock into the pan and boil fast for several minutes, stirring and scraping round the base of the pan to loosen the sediment. Add the tomato purée and garlic, and simmer very gently for several minutes. Adjust the seasoning, and strain over the chicken. Garnish with the tomatoes.

1 chicken, about 1½ kg (3¼ lb) oven-
 ready weight
75 g (3 oz) butter
2 tablespoons oil
6–8 firm tomatoes, skinned
salt and ground black pepper
4 tablespoons white wine
2 tablespoons brandy
4 tablespoons chicken *or* veal stock
2 tablespoons tomato purée
1 clove garlic, peeled and crushed

Serves 6

Poulet aux Poivrons de Francine
Chicken Francine with Sweet Peppers

Finely chop the onions, shallots and garlic. Chop the tomatoes, and halve, de-seed and finely slice the peppers. Heat the butter and oil in a large, heavy saucepan. Dry the chicken joints and brown in the hot fat, turning frequently. Add all the remaining ingredients, except the olives. Cover the pan tightly and simmer very gently for 1–1¼ hours, stirring occasionally. About 5 minutes before serving, arrange the chicken pieces in a large dish and keep hot. Remove the herbs from the pan and add the olives. If too much liquid remains, reduce it by boiling rapidly without the lid for a few minutes. Taste and adjust the seasoning and pour over the chicken. Serve without additional vegetables other than a few boiled potatoes.

3 onions, peeled
3 shallots, peeled
3 cloves garlic, peeled
1 kg (2 lb) really ripe tomatoes,
 skinned *or* 1 kg (2 lb) can peeled
 tomatoes, drained
1 kg (2 lb) mixed sweet red and green
 peppers
50 g (2 oz) butter
2 tablespoons olive oil
1½ kg (3¼ lb) raw chicken joints
2 sprigs thyme
1 tiny piece sage
1 small bay leaf
1 teaspon paprika
pinch cayenne
salt and ground black pepper
100 g (4 oz) *each* black and green olives

Serves 6

Poulet Julienne
Chicken Julienne

Trim the celery, cut away any tough pieces, then slice the rest into large matchsticks. Wash the leeks thoroughly in cold, salted water, drain, and cut across into fairly thin slices. Wipe and quarter the mushrooms. Season the inside of the chicken, insert a few pieces of the celery and 25 g (1 oz) of the butter. Heat the rest of the butter and the oil in a heavy braising pan and brown the chicken on all sides; this will take about 15 minutes. Add the remaining celery, the leeks and mushrooms, then raise the heat for a few minutes without letting the

2 large sticks celery
200 g (8 oz) white part of leeks
300 g (12 oz) mushrooms
1 chicken, 2 kg (generous 4 lb) oven-
 ready weight
salt and ground black pepper
65 g (2½ oz) butter
2 tablespoons oil
2 egg yolks
125 ml (¼ pint) double cream

Serves 8

vegetables colour. Add seasoning, cover the pan, lower the heat and simmer very gently for about 1¼ hours (use an asbestos or wire mat under the pan if necessary). When the chicken is cooked, take it out and keep hot. Strain the vegetables, reserving the liquid, and keeping them hot. Pour off the surface fat then return the liquid to the braising pan and warm up slowly. Whisk the egg yolks and cream together, then whisk quickly into the warm stock and heat gradually until thickened; do not allow to boil. Carve the chicken, arrange on the serving dish and surround with the vegetables. Pour the sauce over and serve at once.

Poulet en Gelée
Cold Jellied Chicken

1 calf's or pig's foot
200 g (8 oz) pork rind without any fat (p. 23)
3 carrots, peeled and halved
3 onions, peeled and halved
2 cloves garlic, peeled
1 sprig thyme
1 bay leaf
3–4 sprigs parsley
250 ml (½ pint) dry white wine
1 chicken, 2 kg (4¼ lb) oven-ready weight, including giblets
salt and ground black pepper
25 g (1 oz) can truffles (optional)
125 g (5½ oz) can purée de foie d'oie truffée

Serves 7 or 8

Ask the butcher to split the calf's or pig's foot in half lengthways. Put all the ingredients down to, and including the wine, into a deep saucepan. Place the chicken and the giblets (except the liver) on top, add salt and pepper and enough water to cover the legs of the chicken. Cover the pan tightly and simmer very gently for 2 hours. Take out the chicken and, when it is cool enough to handle, remove all the skin. Cut off the meat in neat slices and leave to become quite cold. Meanwhile, leave the pan boiling on the stove, uncovered, until the stock has reduced enough to form a solid jelly. Test by putting a spoonful on a saucer in the refrigerator from time to time. When it is ready, strain it through two thicknesses of damp muslin, and leave to cool.

Slice the truffles if used, and turn out the foie d'oie on to a plate. Dip a Charlotte mould in cold water then turn upside down to drain. Line the mould with jelly using the following method. Fill a baking tin with ice cubes. Pour some cold and almost setting jelly into the mould and turn it slowly on the ice until a thick film sets on the sides and bottom of the mould. When set, decorate the bottom with slices of truffle and cover with the best slices of white chicken meat. Spread this with a little foie d'oie and continue in layers, ending with chicken. Pour in cold but liquid jelly to cover, and leave to set in a cold place. Keep a little of the jelly stock in reserve and if there is not enough, make up with water and aspic crystals.

Unmould the chicken some hours before it is needed, and if any of the coating has come away in the unmoulding, pour a little barely liquid stock over it and set aside in a cold place.

Francine wrote: 'This dish, which was always served at my grandmother's house on fête days, is absolutely delicious and very easy to make. It has the advantage, too, of having to be made the day before it is wanted. It is ideal to follow hot soup after the theatre.'

Poulet des Karpates
Chicken Karpates

Season the chicken inside and out and rub the skin generously all over with softened butter. Place it in a plastic roaster bag. Squeeze the lemon juice over the mushrooms and put these into the bag with the onions, shallot and herbs. Tie the open end of the bag securely with string, leaving enough space for the contents to expand. Put the parcel into an ovenproof serving dish. Cook in a moderately hot oven preheated to 190°C, 375°F or Gas Mark 5 for 30 minutes, then turn the parcel over and continue cooking for another 40 minutes. To serve, slit the plastic bag along one side and pull it away, leaving the chicken and vegetables in the serving dish.

1 chicken, about 1¼ kg (2½ lb) oven-ready weight
salt and ground black pepper
40 g (1½ oz) butter
juice of ½ lemon
200 g (8 oz) button mushrooms, washed
2 onions, peeled and chopped
1 shallot, peeled and chopped
1 teaspoon *each* chopped fresh herbs parsley, chives, chervil and tarragon, as available

Serves 4

Poulet Mediterranée
Mediterranean Chicken

Cream the cheese with salt, pepper and spice to taste, and put it into the chicken with one bay leaf. Stand the chicken in a baking tin, brush it thoroughly all over with some of the olive oil, and dust lightly with salt and pepper. Roast in the centre of a moderately hot oven preheated to 190°C, 375°F or Gas Mark 5 for 20 minutes per 450 g (1 lb) and 20 minutes over. After the first 15 minutes of cooking, add half of the vermouth and baste the chicken frequently for the rest of the cooking. Put the carrots into 125 ml (¼-pint) water with the shallot, garlic, remaining bay leaf, and a pinch of salt; cover, and simmer very gently until tender. Heat the olives slowly in another pan with 15 g (½-oz) of the butter and the remaining oil. When the chicken is cooked, carve it and arrange the pieces on a serving dish. Garnish with the drained carrots and the olives, and keep hot in the oven. Skim the fat off the juices in the braising pan, add 175 ml (⅓-pint) boiling water and the rest of the vermouth, boil rapidly for a few minutes, stirring and scraping the bottom of the pan. Cream the remaining 15 g (½-oz) butter with the flour, then add in small pieces to the pan, stirring and boiling for several minutes. Check the seasoning, add the cream and pour into a sauce boat.

2 Petit Suisse cheeses
salt and ground black pepper
about ¼ level teaspoon mixed spice
1 chicken, about 1½ kg (3¼ lb) oven-ready weight
2 bay leaves
2 tablespoons olive oil
175 ml (⅓ pint) dry white vermouth
450 g (1 lb) young carrots, peeled and diced
1 shallot, peeled and chopped
1 clove garlic, peeled and chopped
200 g (8 oz) pitted green olives
25 g (1 oz) butter
2 level teaspoons flour
1 tablespoon double cream

Serves 6 or 7

Poulet Mystère
Mystery Chicken

1 chicken, 2 kg (4¼ lb) oven-ready
   weight, including giblets
salt and ground black pepper
50 g (2 oz) butter
1 tablespoon oil
125 ml (¼ pint) dry white wine
2 tablespoons brandy
200 g (8 oz) button mushrooms,
   washed
500 ml (1 pint) coating Béchamel
   Sauce (p. 33)
about ½ teaspoon Worcestershire
   sauce
2 tablespoons double cream
sprigs of tarragon, chervil *or* parsley
   to garnish

Serves 7 or 8

Season the chicken inside and out. Heat 25 g (1 oz) of the butter and the oil in a heavy oval braising pan and brown the chicken on all sides. Add the giblets, cover the pan tightly, and cook over the lowest possible heat (use an asbestos or wire mat if necessary) for 30 minutes. Add the wine and continue cooking for another 30 minutes. Add the brandy and cook for a further 30 minutes. When the chicken is nearly cooked, put the mushrooms into a pan with the remaining butter and sauté them over low heat until all their liquid has evaporated. Arrange the cooked chicken in a deep serving dish and keep hot in a warm oven. Discard the giblets. Stir the Béchamel Sauce into the pan in which the chicken was cooked, and add Worcestershire sauce and seasoning to taste. When very hot but not boiling, stir in the cream and pour over the chicken. Garnish with sprigs of tarragon, chervil or parsley.

Poulet au Porto à la Crème
Chicken with Port and Cream Sauce

1 chicken, about 1½ kg (3¼ lb) oven-
   ready weight
1 tablespoon oil
50 g (2 oz) butter
salt and ground black pepper
100 ml (scant ¼ pint) water
125 ml (¼ pint) white port
2 egg yolks
125 ml (¼ pint) double cream

Serves 6

Cut the chicken into six pieces. Heat the oil and butter in a sauté pan, add the chicken and turn until the joints are well coated with fat. Add salt and pepper, cover the pan tightly and simmer very gently over low heat for 1 hour (use an asbestos or wire mat if necessary). The butter should not darken and the chicken should be only lightly coloured when it is cooked. Take out the pieces of chicken, cover and keep hot. Pour the water into the sauté pan and boil up while stirring and scraping the pan to loosen any sediment; pour into a bowl and reserve. Pour the port into the sauté pan and boil briskly until reduced by half, then add the reserved stock. Using a wire whisk, mix the egg yolks with the cream, then little by little whisk in the hot, but not boiling, stock. Return to the pan and heat, stirring, until slightly thickened, but do not let it boil. Arrange the chicken on a hot dish and cover with the sauce.

Poulet Quo Vadis
Chicken Quo Vadis

Reserve the giblets, and season the inside of the chicken. Chop the chicken liver. Put the breadcrumbs into a small saucepan with the milk, chicken liver, half of the tarragon, salt, pepper and 25 g (1 oz) of the butter. Stir over low heat until the butter melts and the stuffing binds together. Stuff the neck end of the chicken and re-truss the bird. Place it in a large braising pan with the giblets, onions and water or stock. Cover tightly and simmer gently for $1\frac{1}{4}$–$1\frac{1}{2}$ hours. Remove the chicken and onions and keep hot. Strain the stock. Melt the remaining butter in another saucepan, stir in the flour and cook for a minute or so over low heat, then whisk in a measured 500 ml (1 pint) of the hot stock. Cook, stirring, until the sauce thickens and boils. Whisk the egg yolks, cream, mustard and remaining chopped tarragon together in a basin, then stir about one-third of the hot sauce into it. Return all to the sauce in the pan, and heat very gently without boiling. Check the seasoning and pour into a sauceboat.

Plain boiled rice goes well with this chicken, which can be served whole or ready with the stuffing cut into small pieces.

1 chicken, about $1\frac{1}{2}$ kg ($3\frac{1}{4}$ lb) oven-ready weight, including giblets
salt and ground black pepper
50 g (2 oz) day-old breadcrumbs
5 tablespoons milk
a handful fresh tarragon leaves, chopped
50 g (2 oz) butter
6 small onions, peeled
500 ml (1 pint) water *or* stock
2 level tablespoons plain flour
2 egg yolks
4 tablespoons double cream
$\frac{1}{2}$ level teaspoon made tarragon-flavoured mustard

Serves 6

Poulet en Daube
Casseroled Chicken

Put the bird in a deep basin and add the wine, carrots, onion, garlic, spice, bouquet garni, salt and pepper. Leave to marinate overnight, turning the chicken occasionally before you go to bed. About 5 hours before you plan to eat, take the chicken out of the marinade and wipe it dry. Heat the oil and butter in a large deep saucepan or casserole, and when hot, brown the chicken all over. This will take about 10 minutes Add the pork rind, the wine and vegetables of the marinade (but not the bouquet garni), knuckle of veal or calf's foot, orange peel, thyme, bay leaf, salt and pepper. Cover the pan tightly, and cook over the lowest possible heat (use an asbestos or wire mat if necessary) for 4 hours—during the cooking, the liquid in the pan should barely move. At the end of this time the bird should be very tender. Arrange the chicken on a serving dish and keep hot. If necessary, reduce the sauce by rapid boiling, then skim off the fat, adjust the seasoning and strain into a sauceboat. The chicken can, if liked, be garnished with separately cooked carrots and small onions.

If there is any of this chicken left over after eating it hot, Francine suggested carving it up, pouring the remaining sauce over it and leaving it in a cold place. Next day it will be covered in a perfectly seasoned aspic.

1 boiling fowl, about $2\frac{1}{2}$ kg ($5\frac{1}{4}$ lb) oven-ready weight
500 ml (1 pint) robust red wine
3 carrots, peeled and chopped
1 onion, peeled and chopped
2 cloves garlic, peeled
pinch mixed spice
large Bouquet Garni (p. 22)
salt and ground black pepper
2 tablespoons oil
25 g (1 oz) butter
200 g (8 oz) pork rind, diced (p. 23)
1 knuckle of veal *or* split calf's foot
1 thin strip orange peel
1 sprig thyme
1 small bay leaf

Serves 10

Poulet Rouennaise
Chicken Rouen Style

1½ kg (3¼ lb) chicken joints
100 g (4 oz) butter
salt and ground black pepper
200 g (8 oz) mushrooms
4 tablespoons brandy
250 ml (½ pint) double cream

Serves 6

Dry the chicken joints with kitchen paper. Heat 75 g (3 oz) of the butter in a flameproof casserole and brown the chicken joints all over, turning frequently. Sprinkle with salt and pepper. Cover the pan tightly and put into a moderate oven preheated to 190°C, 375°F or Gas Mark 5. Meanwhile, wash the mushrooms and cut them into thin slices. After the chicken has been in the oven for 30 minutes, add the mushrooms. When the chicken is cooked, take it out of the pan and keep hot. Put the pan, uncovered, on top of the stove and boil for a minute or two to concentrate the juices. Return the chicken. Heat the brandy, ignite and pour flaming over the chicken. When the flames have gone out, stir in the cream, check the seasoning, and simmer very gently for a few minutes, stirring all the time. Arrange the chicken on the serving dish, stir the remaining butter into the sauce and pour it over the chicken.

Poulet au Sel
Chicken Baked in Salt

2 kg (generous 4 lb) coarse kitchen
  salt *or* sea *or* rock salt
1 free range chicken, about 1¼–1½ kg
  (3 lb) oven-ready weight

Serves 6

Divide the salt into three equal portions. Choose a heavy oval ovenproof casserole into which the chicken will just fit comfortably. Spread one portion of salt over the bottom of the casserole, put the chicken on it, arrange another portion of salt all round the chicken, and cover with the remainder. The bird must be completely surrounded and covered with salt. Cover the casserole tightly. Cook in the centre of a hot oven preheated to 200°C, 400°F or Gas Mark 6 for about 1½ hours. When you open the casserole you will find the salt has formed a crust. Break this away carefully so that the chicken skin, now golden brown and crisp, will not be torn. Unbelievable as it may seem, chicken cooked in this way is not in the least salty but simply delicious. As it is cooked without fat it is a perfect dish for those on a fat-free diet.

When Francine was cooking, salt cost only a few old pence per pound. Nowadays the salt can be kept and re-used.

Suprêmes de Volaille Noisette
Chicken Breasts Cooked in Butter

4 chicken breasts
a little flour
salt and ground black pepper
100 g (4 oz) unsalted butter
1 tablespoon oil
2 tablespoons finely chopped parsley
1 tablespoon lemon juice

Serves 4

Remove any skin and bones from the chicken breasts. Place them between greaseproof paper and beat to flatten them. Season the flour with salt and pepper, coat the chicken breasts evenly and press the coating on firmly. Heat 50 g (2 oz) of the butter and the oil in a large frying pan and when hot fry the chicken breasts over moderate heat for 3–4 minutes each side, until cooked through and golden. Remove to a hot dish. If the fat has become at all discoloured, discard it. Put the remaining butter into the pan, heat until beginning to turn brown and smell 'nutty', then remove it and stir in the parsley and lemon juice. Pour over the chicken and serve at once. Provençale Stuffed Tomatoes (p. 77) and green beans go well with this dish.

Coq au Vin Rouge
Chicken in Red Wine

Cut the chicken in half, cut off the backbone, leg shanks, wing tips and parson's nose, and put these into a saucepan with the giblets (except the liver) Add the onion, bay leaf, a little salt and pepper and cold water just to cover, then simmer, covered, for 45 minutes or pressure cook for 15 minutes. Strain and reserve the stock.

Cut the chicken into six joints and pat them dry with kitchen paper. Cut the pork into 1 cm (⅓-inch) strips. Heat 25 g (1 oz) of the butter and the oil in a wide flameproof casserole and fry the chicken joints, pork strips and button onions until golden, turning as necessary. Add the garlic, herbs and seasoning, cover the pan and cook over low heat for 10 minutes, shaking the pan from time to time. Drain off any surplus fat. Pour the brandy into a heated ladle, ignite and pour over the chicken. Shake the pan gently until the flames die down. Add the wine and reserved stock, and when boiling, cover the pan tightly and transfer to the centre of a moderate oven preheated to 180°C, 350°F or Gas Mark 4 for 1 hour.

Remove the chicken joints, onions and pork, and keep warm. Discard the herbs. Boil the liquid rapidly until reduced to about 250 ml (½-pint). Cream the flour with 25 g (1 oz) of the butter to a paste (this is known as *beurre manié*, used for thickening liquids) and add to the pan in walnut sized pieces, whisking briskly all the time until the sauce thickens to a light coating consistency. Check the seasoning and replace the chicken, onions and pork, and heat gently for 10 minutes.

Quickly sauté the mushroom caps in the remaining butter and prepare the croûtons of fried bread if used.

Arrange the chicken, onions and pork in a shallow gratin dish, pour the sauce over them and garnish with the button mushrooms, croûtons and chopped parsley.

1 chicken, about 1½ kg (3¼ lb) oven-
  ready weight, including giblets
1 small onion, peeled and sliced
½ bay leaf
salt and ground black pepper
100 g (4 oz) sliced pickled pork
75 g (3 oz) butter
1 tablespoon oil
12 button onions, peeled
1 clove garlic, peeled and crushed
Bouquet Garni (p. 22)
2 tablespoons brandy
½ bottle robust red wine
25 g (1 oz) flour
150 g (6 oz) button mushrooms,
  washed and dried
Garnish
diamond-shaped croûtons of fried
  bread
a little chopped parsley

Serves 6

Canard aux Cerises
Cold Duck with Cherries

1 litre (2 pint) pack aspic jelly crystals
1 cold roast duck, about 2¼ kg
  (5 lb) raw oven-ready weight
450 g (1 lb) ripe red cherries
200 g (8 oz) ripe black cherries *or*
  black grapes

Serves 5 or 6

Make up the aspic jelly as instructed and set aside until cold but not set. Carve all the meat off the duck in neat slices and arrange them in a gratin dish large enough to take all the duck in one layer (or use two dishes). Barely cover the duck with aspic jelly and leave in a cool place to set. Stone the cherries carefully without spoiling their shape. De-seed the grapes if used.) When the aspic has set, lift off with the point of a knife any specks of grease which may have risen to the surface. Arrange a ring of red cherries round the edge of the dish and criss-cross the surface with alternate rows of red and black cherries (or grapes). Pour a layer of barely liquid aspic (i.e. on the point of setting) over all and leave in a cool place to set.

Canard à l'Ananas
Duck with Pineapple

1 duck, 2 kg (4½ lb) oven-ready
  weight, including giblets
salt and ground black pepper
25 g (1 oz) butter
1 tablespoon oil
1 medium sized ripe fresh pineapple

Serves 4 or 5

Remove the giblets from the duck and season the inside with salt and pepper. Prick the skin with a fork. Heat the butter and oil in an oval braising pan and brown the duck all over. Add the giblets (except the liver), cover, and transfer the casserole to a moderate oven preheated to 180°C, 350°F or Gas Mark 4. Cook for 25 minutes per 450 g (1 lb) weight. Meanwhile, cut the top off the pineapple, scoop out the flesh, cut away all tough parts and chop the rest into small pieces.

When the duck is cooked, remove it from the pan and keep hot. Discard the giblets. Pour the juices into a very cold basin and remove the fat as it rises to the top. Pour the gravy from beneath the fat back into the pan, add the pieces of pineapple and heat slowly. Arrange the duck on a serving dish and pour the gravy and pineapple around it.

Canard aux Navets
Duck with Turnips

1 leek
1 carrot, peeled
1 onion, peeled
duck's giblets
1 Bouquet Garni (p. 22)
salt and ground black pepper
1 duck, 2 kg (4½ lb) oven-ready
  weight, including giblets
2 tablespoons oil
6–8 button onions, peeled
700 g (1½ lb) turnips, peeled
75 g (3 oz) butter
2 tablespoons caster sugar
25 g (1 oz) flour

Serves 4 or 5

Trim the leek and wash very thoroughly in cold salted water. Roughly chop the leek, carrot and onion and put with the duck giblets, bouquet garni, salt and pepper and 500 ml (1 pint) water into a saucepan. Bring slowly to the boil and simmer, covered, for about 1 hour or until reduced to 250 ml (½-pint); strain and reserve. Season the inside of the duck, and prick the skin with a fork. Heat the oil in a heavy braising pan and brown the duck on all sides over moderate heat. Add the button onions, cover the pan and transfer to a moderate oven preheated to 180°C, 350°F or Gas Mark 4. Cook for 25 minutes per 450 g (1 lb) weight. Meanwhile cut the turnips into small sticks and put into a heavy saucepan with 50 g (2 oz) of the butter, salt and pepper. Cover tightly and cook over the lowest possible heat (use an asbestos or wire mat if necessary) for 20 minutes, shaking the pan frequently. Now dust the turnips with the sugar, cover, and continue cooking slowly, stirring frequently, until tender and nicely glazed. Melt the remaining 25 g (1 oz) butter in a saucepan, add the flour and cook gently for several minutes, stirring until pale brown. Little by little, stir in the strained stock and continue stirring until boiling and thickened. Season to taste. Remove the duck from the braising pan and keep hot. Pour the liquid from the pan into a very cold basin and remove the fat as it rises to the top. Add the gravy from beneath the fat to the sauce, and reheat. Place the duck on a serving dish, arrange the turnips round it, and pour the sauce over.

Pintades au Porto
Guinea Fowl with Port

Set aside the livers of the guinea fowl. Mash the garlic with the herbs then beat into the cheese. Put one half into each bird. Melt the butter in a flameproof oval casserole, put in the guinea fowl and brown on all sides. Sprinkle with salt and pepper, transfer to a moderate oven preheated to 190°C, 375°F or Gas Mark 5 and roast for 45 minutes to 1 hour. After 30 minutes' cooking, heat the brandy, light it and pour flaming over the birds. When the flame has gone out, pour in half of the port and baste the birds frequently for the remainder of the cooking time. Meanwhile, heat the oil in a small saucepan and fry the shallots until golden. Chop the reserved livers and add, stirring and cooking for several minutes. Add salt, pepper, nutmeg, the truffle peelings and their juice if used, and the remaining port; simmer gently for 15 minutes. Lift out the fowl, carve them and arrange on a serving dish. Add the liver sauce to the juices in the casserole in which the birds were cooked, then the cream and pour over the guinea fowl.

2 guinea fowl, about 1 kg (2 lb)
    each, oven-ready weight
2 cloves garlic, peeled
1 teaspoon mixed chopped rosemary,
    savory and marjoram
2 Petit Suisse cheeses
50 g (2 oz) butter
salt and ground black pepper
4 tablespoons brandy
12 tablespoons port
2 tablespoons oil
4 shallots, peeled and sliced
pinch grated nutmeg
15 g (½ oz) can truffle peelings
    (optional)
1 tablespoon double cream

Serves 6–8

Pigeonneaux à la Normand
Normandy Style Pigeons

Heat the oil and 30 g (generous 1 oz) of the butter in a wide flameproof casserole and brown the pigeons well all over, turning frequently. Peel and core the apples, slice three of them into ½-cm (¼-inch) thick rings and cut the other two into quarters. Heat the remaining butter in a large frying pan and fry the apple slices gently until golden, turning once. When the pigeons are browned, take them out of the casserole and put

1 tablespoon oil
65 g (2½ oz) butter
4 young pigeons, plucked and drawn
5 large dessert apples
salt and ground black pepper
2 teaspoons Calvados
250 ml (½ pint) double cream

Serves 4

the apple slices in, making a bed on the base of the pan. Arrange the pigeons on the bed of apple, surround with apple quarters and season lightly. Cover the casserole tightly, and transfer to a moderate oven preheated to 180°C, 350°F or Gas Mark 4 for 1–1¼ hours. When the pigeons are cooked, arrange on a serving dish with the apple between them and around. Add the Calvados and cream to the sauté pan, heat, whisking vigorously but do not let it boil. Check the seasoning and pour over the pigeons.

Pigeonneaux à la Catalan
Pigeons Catalan

4 young pigeons, plucked and drawn
100 g (4 oz) Parma ham*
4 sprigs fresh parsley
1 clove garlic, peeled and crushed
salt and ground black pepper
1 egg, beaten
4 thin strips barding fat (p. 21)
25 g (1 oz) butter
1 tablespoon oil
1 level tablespoon flour
125 ml (¼ pint) dry white wine
250 ml (½ pint) chicken *or* veal stock
1 tablespoon tomato purée
1 sprig thyme
1 bay leaf
1 thin strip orange peel
extra cloves garlic, to taste

Serves 4
*a delicately cured raw ham; lean
  gammon is the nearest substitute

Finely chop the pigeons' livers with 50 g (2 oz) of the ham and 2 sprigs of parsley. Add the garlic, salt and pepper and the egg; mix thoroughly. Stuff the pigeons with this mixture, then tie a piece of barding fat over the breast of each bird. Melt the butter and oil in a flameproof casserole and brown the pigeons all over. Remove them from the pan. Cut the remaining ham into 1 cm (⅓-inch) pieces and sauté in the same pan. Stir in the flour and cook for a minute, then stir in the wine and stock and all the remaining ingredients except the extra cloves of garlic. Cover, and simmer for 10 minutes. Remove the pieces of ham, strain the sauce and adjust the seasoning. Return the sauce to the pan and add the ham and pigeons. Cover, and simmer for 10 minutes.

Francine said that to follow the regional recipe scrupulously, you would boil 12 peeled cloves of garlic in salted water for 10 minutes, drain, then add to the pigeons. Four cloves are enough for most tastes; but add them only if you feel inclined. Continue simmering the dish, covered, until the pigeons are cooked (another 45 minutes to 1 hour at least). Serve from the casserole.

Pigeonneaux aux Raisins Secs
Pigeons with Raisins

150 g (6 oz) large raisins
4 medium onions, peeled
75 g (3 oz) butter
2 tablespoons oil
4 young pigeons, plucked and drawn
1–2 shakes cayenne
salt and ground black pepper

Serves 4

Cover the raisins with tepid water and soak for 2 hours, then split open and remove the seeds; leave to drain. Finely slice the onions. Heat 50 g (2 oz) of the butter in a frying pan and very gently fry the onions, stirring frequently, until they begin to soften. Heat the remaining 25 g (1 oz) butter and the oil in a wide flameproof casserole and brown the pigeons on all sides. Add the onions, raisins, cayenne, salt and pepper. Cover the pan tightly and cook over *very low* heat until tender, stirring now and then. This will take from 1 to 1½ hours. Serve from casserole.

Pigeons aux Petits Pois
Pigeons with Peas

Cut the belly pork into thin strips. Heat the oil and butter in a large flameproof casserole, and fry the pork strips and button onions over low heat for 5–10 minutes until golden, stirring frequently. Remove from the pan with a slotted spoon. Fry the pigeons gently until lightly browned all over. Add the wine and allow to bubble briskly for a minute or so, then add the stock and bring to the boil. Return the bacon and onions to the pan, add the peas, shredded lettuce, bouquet garni and seasonings of salt, pepper and sugar. Cover the pan tightly and simmer very gently for 1¼–1½ hours, until the pigeons are tender.

To serve, discard the bouquet garni and serve from the casserole, allowing half a pigeon for each person.

150 g (6 oz) sliced belly pork
1 tablespoon oil
25 g (1 oz) butter
18 button onions, peeled
3 young pigeons, plucked and drawn
125 ml (¼ pint) white wine
125 ml (¼ pint) chicken stock
450 g (1 lb) shelled peas, fresh or
    frozen
1 lettuce, washed and shredded
1 Bouquet Garni (p. 22)
salt and ground black pepper
1 teaspoon sugar

Serves 6

Ramiers aux Raisins Noirs
Wood Pigeons with Black Grapes

Prepare the marinade, and marinate the pigeons in it for 48 hours, turning them over from time to time. Reserve marinade. Leave in a cool place. When ready to cook, melt the butter in a heavy saucepan, add the shallots and carrot and start frying them. Drain the pigeons from the reserved marinade, dry them, put in the pan with the shallots and carrot and fry until lightly browned on all sides. Heat the whisky, light it and pour flaming over the pigeons. When the flames have gone out, take the pigeons out of the pan, strain the marinade into it and boil rapidly for a few minutes to reduce. Return the pigeons to the pan, add salt and pepper, cover the pan tightly and simmer *gently* until cooked. The time will depend on the age of the pigeons, but will probably be from 1 to 1½ hours. Meanwhile, put half of the grapes through the finest mesh of a vegetable mill, or press through a sieve. When ready to serve, prepare the buttered toast and remove the crusts. Put a slice of ham on each and a drained pigeon on top of the ham. Add the grape purée to the sauce and reduce by rapid boiling for a few minutes. Check the seasoning. Garnish the pigeons with the whole grapes and serve the sauce separately.

Basic Marinade, half quantity (p. 28)
4 young wood pigeons, plucked and
    drawn
50 g (2 oz) butter
4 small shallots, peeled and sliced
1 small carrot, peeled and sliced
4 tablespoons whisky
salt and ground black pepper
200 g (8 oz) black grapes
4 slices buttered toast
4 thin slices cooked ham

Serves 4

Dinde Rôtie
Roast Stuffed Turkey

1 turkey about 4½ kg (10 lb) oven-
ready weight, including liver
8 tablespoons medium sherry
25 g (10 z) can truffles (optional)
450 g (1 lb) chestnuts
300 g (12 oz) lean gammon, minced
salt and ground black pepper
200 g (8 oz) barding fat (p. 21)

Serves 12–15

Chop the turkey liver and marinate for as long as possible in the sherry. Chop the truffles, if used, and add to the marinade. With a sharp knife, make a slit in the skin of each chestnut. Half cook the chestnuts in boiling salted water, then drain and peel, keeping them as whole as possible. Strain off and reserve the sherry marinade, then mix the chopped liver and truffle with the minced gammon, chestnuts, salt and pepper. Stuff the neck end of the turkey with this mixture, re-truss and brush it all over with the sherry. Cover the breast and legs with thin slices of barding fat. Stand the bird on a trivet in a baking tin, and roast in the centre of a moderate oven preheated to 180°C, 350°F or Gas Mark 4 until cooked (about 3½–4 hours). While cooking, baste the bird occasionally, and 20 minutes before it is ready, remove the barding fat to allow the breast to brown.

L'Oie de Noël
Christmas Goose

truffles (see recipe)
125 ml (¼ pint) Madeira
1 goose weighing about 4½ kg (9–10 lb), including liver
2¾ kg (6 lb) chestnuts
salt and pepper

Serves 10–12, even at Christmas

Truffles are necessary in this recipe. But as their flavour is pervasive, a small amount will suffice. Use as much as you can afford. Truffle peelings are ideal.

Tip the truffles into the Madeira, bring slowly to the boil, and boil for a few minutes. Put into a bowl, add the goose liver and leave to marinate all night.

Remove all the fat you can from inside the goose and set it aside.

Peel the chestnuts, then put some of the goose fat into a saucepan, add the chestnuts, cover the pan and simmer for 1 hour, adding more fat from time to time as it is needed.

Chop the liver and chestnuts and slice the truffles. Set some of the best truffle slices aside for a garnish, but add the others to the liver and chestnuts, moisten with the Madeira, add salt and pepper and stuff the goose. (Some cooks add chopped veal or pork to the stuffing, but Francine preferred it as given here, although sometimes adding 2 cooking apples very finely chopped.)

Sew up the goose and roast it in the oven according to its weight (about 3 hours). Baste frequently, but remove excess fat from the pan from time to time as the bird should not lie in too much grease.

Perdrix aux Raisins
Partridge with Grapes

*Partridges are in season from September to January inclusive, and at their best in October and November. The birds should be hung before dressing.

Prepare a hot oven preheated to 200°C, 400°F or Gas Mark 6. Skin and de-seed half of the grapes, leaving them whole if possible. Season the birds inside with salt and pepper, and insert about 10 g ($\frac{1}{3}$-oz) butter and a few de-seeded grapes into each. Melt the remaining butter and the oil in a flameproof casserole and brown the birds lightly all over. Arrange the birds breast down in the casserole, cover, and cook in the centre of the oven for 30–40 minutes or until tender. Press the *unpeeled* grapes through a sieve.

When the birds are cooked, lift them from the pan, discard the trussing string and arrange them on a serving dish; keep warm. Pour the grape juice into the buttery juices in the casserole, add the lemon juice and the remaining peeled grapes. Heat gently without boiling and check the seasoning. Spoon the grapes round the birds and pour the sauce over them.

450 g (1 lb) white grapes
3 young partridges, oven-ready*
salt and ground black pepper
65 g (2$\frac{1}{2}$ oz) butter
1 tablespoon oil
2 teaspoons lemon juice

Serves 6

Perdrix aux Choux
Partridge with Cabbage

This is a classic French way of cooking old partridges. Cut the cabbage into quarters. Put them into a saucepan of cold water, bring to the boil, cook for 2–3 minutes and then drain. Repeat this process once more. Cabbage is more easily digested if it is blanched twice in this way.

Cut the bacon into 1 cm ($\frac{1}{3}$-inch) cubes. Put the butter and bacon into a flameproof casserole and heat gently until the bacon fat is running freely. Raise the heat, put in the partridges and brown all over. Take off the heat and add the carrots, onion, bouquet garni, cabbage, wine, brandy and salt and pepper. Cover the casserole tightly and cook in the centre of a slow oven preheated to 170°C, 325°F or Gas Mark 3 for 1$\frac{1}{2}$–2 hours depending on the age of the birds.

To serve, take out the birds and halve them; discard the bouquet garni. Roughly chop the cabbage with the rest of the contents of the pan, arrange these in a deep serving dish and place the halved birds on top.

1 kg (2 lb) hard white cabbage
300 kg (12 oz) piece unsmoked **streaky** bacon
25 g (1 oz) butter
2 casserole partridges, oven-ready
2 carrots, peeled and sliced
1 onion, peeled and quartered
1 Bouquet Garni (p. 22)
125 ml ($\frac{1}{4}$ pint) white wine
2 tablespoons brandy
salt and ground black pepper

Serves 4

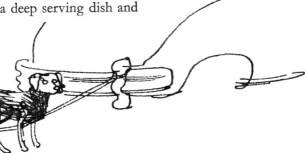

Faisan à la Bohémienne
Gipsy Pheasant

*Pheasants are in season from October to February and at their best during November to December. An average weight is ¾-1 kg (1½-2 lb), serving 3-4 portions. To develop their gamey flavour, birds should be hung for 7-10 days before dressing

1 young pheasant, oven-ready*
salt and ground black pepper
1 bay leaf
1 sprig *each* thyme and tarragon
5 small shallots
75 g (3 oz) butter
3 tablespoons brandy
250 ml (½ pint) veal *or* chicken stock
1 clove garlic, peeled
2 slices fat ham
4 chicken livers, about 50 g (2 oz)
1 egg yolk
1 level teaspoon paprika
4 large squares buttered toast, crusts removed
4 tablespoons double cream

Serves 3 or 4

If the pheasant's liver is available, keep this on one side. Dust the inside of the bird with salt and pepper and insert the bay leaf, thyme and tarragon.

Cut two of the shallots in half and put into a small flame-proof casserole with 40 g (1½ oz) of the butter. Heat gently on top of the cooker and when hot put in the pheasant and brown lightly all over. Pour the brandy into a heated ladle, light it and pour flaming over the pheasant. Shake the casserole gently until the flames die down. Turn the bird breast side downwards and add the stock and a little seasoning. Transfer the casserole to the centre of a moderate oven preheated to 180°C, 350°F or Gas Mark 4 and cook until tender, basting frequently, about 45–50 minutes.

Meanwhile, finely chop the remaining shallots and the garlic and ham. Heat 25 g (1 oz) of the butter in a small saucepan, add the chicken livers, the pheasant liver if available, the chopped shallots, garlic and ham, and a little pepper. Cover, and simmer very gently for 10 minutes, stirring now and then. Mash the contents to a paste, or pass through a fine vegetable mill. Stir in the egg yolk, paprika and the remaining butter. Cover, and keep hot by standing in a larger pan of near-boiling water.

When the pheasant is tender, take it out of the pan and carve into four portions. Prepare the toast, spread with the liver mixture and arrange a portion of pheasant on top of each.

Heat the casserole in which the pheasant was cooked on top of the stove, scraping the pan to loosen any sediment, and if necessary boiling rapidly until reduced to about 175 ml (⅓-pint) Stir in the cream, check the seasoning and serve this sauce separately.

Faisan en Compôte
Casserole of Pheasant

1 casserole pheasant, oven-ready*
25 g (1 oz) butter
2 tablespoons oil
6 shallots, peeled
1 small sprig thyme
salt and ground black pepper
3 tablespoons brandy
250 ml (½ pint) double cream

Serves 3 or 4
*see above

Cut the pheasant into four joints. Put it into a heavy oven-proof casserole with the butter, oil, shallots (whole), thyme and seasonings of salt and pepper. Cover the pan tightly and cook in the centre of a slow oven 150°C, 300°F or Gas Mark 2 for at least 1½ hours (longer if necessary, depending on the age of the bird) but after 1 hour add the brandy and, after 1¼ hours the cream.

When tender stir the sauce briskly to amalgamate the ingredients, check the seasoning, and serve the pheasant from the casserole.

Faisan Braisé Ali-Baba
Braised Pheasant Ali-Baba

Heat 25 g (1 oz) butter in a flameproof casserole a little larger than the pheasant. Add the shallots and pheasant and brown the bird lightly all over. Heat the brandy, light it, pour over the pheasant and shake the pan to distribute the flames. When the flames die, season the bird with salt and pepper and add the stock. Cover the casserole and transfer to the centre of a moderate oven preheated to 180°C, 350°F or Gas Mark 4. Cook for 30 minutes, spooning the liquid over the bird from time to time.

Remove the bird from the casserole, and whisk the cream, vinegar and horseradish into the juices remaining in the pan. Put the pheasant back, baste, cover the pan and return to the oven for another 20–30 minutes, depending on the size of the bird.

Meanwhile, cook the peas according to the instructions on the packet. Melt the remaining 25 g (1 oz) butter and sauté the mushrooms gently for 10 minutes, shaking the pan frequently.

Arrange the pheasant on a serving dish and surround with the drained peas, and the mushrooms. Adjust the seasoning of the sauce and serve it separately.

50 g (2 oz) butter
2 tablespoons finely chopped shallots
1 young pheasant, oven-ready*
2 tablespoons brandy
salt and ground black pepper
125 ml (¼ pint) veal or chicken stock
250 ml (½ pint) double cream
2 tablespoons wine vinegar
1–2 level tablespoons grated horse-radish
300 g (12 oz) frozen peas
200 g (8 oz) button mushrooms, washed

Serves 3 or 4
*see above

Faisan à la Romanoff
Pheasant Romanoff

This is an excellent recipe for cooking a pheasant on top of the cooker.

Dust inside of the pheasant with salt, pepper and a little of the paprika, and insert the cheese. Heat the butter and oil in a heavy based saucepan and slowly brown the pheasant all over —it should be well browned, but the butter must not blacken. Sprinkle with salt and pepper, add the vodka, light it and shake the pan gently to distribute the flames. When the flames die, sprinkle in the remaining paprika, and add the bay leaf and shallot. Arrange the pheasant on its side, add the sherry, cover the pan tightly and simmer very gently for about 30 minutes. Turn the pheasant, add the mushrooms, cover, and continue cooking very gently until the pheasant is cooked, another 30–45 minutes, depending on the age and size of the bird.

Prepare the fried bread and set on a flat serving dish. Lift the pheasant from the pan, discard the trussing string and set

1 young pheasant, oven-ready*
salt and ground black pepper
3 level teaspoons paprika
1 Petit Suisse cheese
25 g (1 oz) butter
1 tablespoon oil
3 tablespoons vodka
½ bay leaf
1 large shallot, peeled and halved
4 tablespoons sweet sherry
300 g (12 oz) button mushrooms, washed
2 large slices fried bread
125 g (¼ pint) double cream

Serves 3 or 4
*(See p. 106)

the bird on the fried bread. Remove the mushrooms and shallot from the pan with a slotted spoon and arrange round the pheasant. Discard the bay leaf. Stir the cream into the juices remaining in the pan, adding a little more sherry, or some stock, if the sauce is too thick. Bring to the boil, pour a little over the pheasant and serve the rest separately.

Faisan Normand
Pheasant Normandy Style

50 g (2 oz) butter
1 tablespoon oil
1 young pheasant, oven-ready*
4 tablespoons Calvados†
1 small shallot, peeled and quartered
1 small carrot, peeled and quartered
1 clove garlic, peeled and quartered
½ bay leaf
salt and ground black pepper
125 ml (¼ pint) white wine *or* dry cider
3 large cooking apples
4 small pieces toast
4 thin slices pickled belly pork
125 ml (¼ pint) double cream

Serves 3 or 4
*see p. 106
†Calvados is apple brandy from Normandy. If not available substitute ordinary brandy

Heat 25 g (1 oz) of the butter with the oil in a heavy based saucepan and slowly brown the pheasant all over—the butter must not blacken. Pour in the Calvados, light it, and when the flame has gone out, add the shallot, carrot and garlic, and continue cooking until they are lightly coloured. Add the bay leaf and salt and pepper, then stir in the wine *or* cider by degrees. Cover the pan tightly and simmer very gently for 1–1¼ hours according to the bird's age and size. The pheasant is cooked when the juices are no longer pink.

Meanwhile, peel, core and quarter the apples, put into a saucepan with 2 tablespoons of water and the remaining butter. Cover, and cook until pulped, then uncover and cook until reduced to a purée; keep warm.

Prepare the toast and cut into oblongs the same size as the slices of belly pork. Set the pieces of pork on the toast and grill gently for 10 minutes or so, until the fat is running and the pork beginning to frizzle.

When the pheasant is cooked, lift it on to a hot serving dish and remove the trussing string. Arrange small mounds of apple purée and the pieces of pork on toast round it

Strain the liquid from the pheasant pan, discard the solids and return the liquid to the pan. If the liquid has reduced very much, add a little cold water, wine or cider, and bring to the boil while scraping around the pan. Whisk in the cream, adjust the seasoning, and bring to the boil, still whisking. Serve the sauce separately.

Bécasses en Cocotte
Woodcock in a Casserole

25 g (1 oz) butter
1 tablespoon oil
4 fresh woodcock, oven-ready*
salt and ground black pepper
4 slices fried bread
3 tablespoons brandy
5 tablespoons game *or* veal stock
watercress to garnish

Serves 4

108

*Woodcock available in Britain are often small and served as a single portion. Larger birds can be halved for two portions. Woodcock should be eaten freshly caught and are plucked and trussed but *not* drawn. Only the gizzard is removed. The 'trail' is considered a great delicacy. Although in season from mid August to January, they are at their best in October and November. A good game merchant will supply oven-ready woodcock with a thin piece of barding fat tied over the breast; otherwise this must be added by the cook.

Prepare a hot oven preheated to 220°C, 425°F or Gas Mark 7. Heat the butter and oil in a flameproof casserole and brown the birds all over. Sprinkle with salt and pepper and arrange them breast side up in the casserole. Cover tightly, transfer to the oven and cook for 20–25 minutes. The meat should be slightly pink as woodcock must on no account be overcooked.

Meanwhile, prepare the pieces of fried bread and arrange on hot serving plates. As soon as the birds are cooked, remove the trussing strings and arrange the birds on the fried bread; keep hot. Pour the brandy and stock into the casserole and boil briskly for a minute or so while stirring and scraping the pan well; check the seasoning and pour into a sauce boat.

Garnish the birds with watercress and serve immediately.

Bécassines sur Petits Poufs
Snipe on Cushions

*Snipe from a reputable game merchant, should be young, fresh birds plucked but not drawn as the 'trail' is considered a delicacy. If they do not have a thin piece of barding fat tied over the breast, this must be added by the cook otherwise the birds may be dry. Snipe are in season from mid August to January, but at their best in October and November. Allow at least one per person.

Prepare a hot oven preheated to 220°C, 425°F or Gas Mark 7. Heat 25 g (1 oz) of the butter and the oil in a heavy based casserole and quickly brown the snipe all over.

Arrange them breast uppermost in the casserole, transfer to the preheated oven and cook, uncovered, for 15–20 minutes, basting several times. The meat should remain a rosy pink.

Meanwhile, wash and dry the chicken livers and discard any discoloured parts. Melt 25 g (1 oz) of the butter in a small saucepan and sauté the livers for 1–2 minutes until they stiffen. Mash them thoroughly with a fork, add 1 tablespoon of the brandy, a little salt and pepper, cover, and cook gently for another 1–2 minutes. Prepare the fried bread, spread with the remaining butter and then with the chicken livers. Arrange on the serving plates.

As soon as the snipe are cooked set one on each piece of bread. Stir 2 tablespoons of water into the pan in which the livers were cooked, bring to the boil and tip into the pan in which the snipe were cooked; add another 2 tablespoons of water and the remaining brandy. Boil for a minute or so, stirring and scraping the pan well. Pour over the birds and serve immediately.

75 g (3 oz) butter
1 tablespoon oil
4 fresh snipe, oven-ready*
100 g (4 oz) chicken livers
3 tablespoons brandy
salt and ground black pepper
4 pieces of fried bread

Serves 4

Canard Sauvage Atomium
Wild Duck Atomium

*Wild duck are in season from mid August to January but at their best in October and November. Usually only the breast of roast wild duck is served.

3 large oranges, seedless if possible
1 large lemon
2 young wild ducks, oven-ready*
salt and ground black pepper
65 g (2½ oz) butter
3 tablespoons brandy
2 tablespoons wine vinegar
2 rounded tablespoons caster sugar
1 tablespoon potato flour
2 tablespoons Grand Marnier *or* Curaçao

Serves 4

Pare the rind very thinly from one of the oranges and from the lemon. Dust the insides of the ducks with seasoning, then put a strip of orange rind and 15 g (½-oz) butter into each.

Preheat a moderately hot oven 190°C, 375°F or Gas Mark 5. Put the remaining butter into a small roasting tin and put in the oven to melt. When the butter is hot, put in the ducks and baste them well. Roast for 30–35 minutes, basting frequently.

Cut the pared orange rind and lemon rind into fine matchsticks. Peel all the white pith from the pared orange and the lemon, remove any pips and put the fruit through the finest vegetable mill. Peel and cut the remaining two oranges into thin slices; reserve for garnishing.

When the ducks are cooked, pour the brandy into a heated ladle, light it and pour flaming over the ducks. Shake the pan gently, and when the flames die remove the ducks to a serving dish and keep hot.

Put the vinegar and sugar into a small heavy based pan. Heat gently until the sugar dissolves, then boil until caramelized. *Immediately* stir the juices from the roasting tin into it and heat gently until the caramel dissolves. Return to the roasting tin, add the potato flour mixed to a smooth cream with 2 tablespoons cold water, and bring to the boil, stirring all the time. Add the puréed fruit and juice and the matchsticks of rind. Heat gently, and add the liqueur at the last moment.

To serve, pour this sauce over the ducks and garnish with the orange slices.

Civet de Lièvre
Hare Stewed in Wine

1 young hare, about 3½ kg (7½ lb)
3–4 juniper berries (optional)
Basic Marinade (p. 28)
50 g (2 oz) butter
40 g (1½ oz) flour
salt and ground black pepper
2 tablespoons double cream

Serves 6–8

Have the hare skinned and paunched and cut into joints. Add the juniper berries, if used, to the marinade. Put the hare joints and the offal (lung, heart and liver) into a deep china basin and add the marinade. Leave in a cool place for 2–3 days, turning the pieces fairly often.

Remove the pieces of hare and dry them. Strain the marinade, and mince the offal.

Melt the butter in a heavy, flameproof casserole, add the pieces of hare and brown them all over; this will take about 15 minutes. Remove them from the pan, stir in the flour and cook, stirring, for a few minutes until lightly browned. Stir in the marinade smoothly, little by little, and bring to the boil.

Season, and replace the hare. Cover the pan tightly and simmer very gently for 30 minutes. Add the minced offal, and continue simmering very gently for another 30–45 minutes, or until tender.

Remove the pieces of hare to a serving dish, stir the cream into the sauce, check the seasoning, and pour over the hare.

Lapin en Compôte
Casseroled Rabbit

Roughly chop the carrots, shallots, garlic and bacon. Wash and dry the rabbit pieces. Heat the butter and oil in a large heavy flameproof casserole and brown the rabbit pieces all over. Add the chopped vegetables, the bacon, and the bouquet garni; sauté lightly for a minute or two, stirring frequently. Add the calf's foot or pig's feet, the wine and generous seasonings of salt and pepper. Cover the pan tightly and simmer very gently for 2–2½ hours, until the rabbit flesh comes easily away from the bones.

Take the rabbit out of the pan and remove the bones. Put the pieces of meat into a fairly deep dish. Remove the feet and bouquet garni and pour the rest of the contents of the pan over the rabbit.

Rabbit done in this way will set in a firm jelly if left to get cold, and is delicious.

3 medium carrots, peeled
3 shallots, peeled
2 or 3 cloves garlic, peeled
150 g (6 oz) absolutely lean bacon
2 kg (4¼ lb) cut rabbit pieces
50 g (2 oz) butter
2 tablespoons oil
1 Bouquet Garni (p. 22) including 1
   sprig savory
1 calf's foot *or* 2 pig's feet, halved
generous ½ litre (1 pint) rosé wine
salt and ground black pepper

Serves 8

Lapin de Garenne à la Moutarde
Wild Rabbit with Mustard

Cut the head off the rabbit and reserve, with the offal, in the refrigerator. Spread the rabbit thickly with mustard and leave in a cool place for 24 hours.

Roughly chop all the vegetables. Put them into a saucepan with the wine, bouquet garni, rabbit head and offal, water and seasoning. Cover tightly and simmer very gently for 1 hour, or pressure cook for 20 minutes. Strain the stock.

Meanwhile, put the tarragon inside the rabbit and then wrap the rabbit completely in the pork rind, securing with a skewer if necessary. Put into a baking tin and cook in a moderate oven preheated to 180°C, 350°F or Gas Mark 4 for about 1 hour.

When the rabbit is ready, discard the pork rind, arrange the rabbit on a serving dish, and keep hot. Add 2 tablespoons cold water to the baking tin and bring to the boil, stirring and scraping the tin. Add the stock and boil for a minute or two then remove the tin from the cooker and stir in the cream. Pour the sauce over the rabbit just before serving.

Plain boiled rice goes well with this dish.

1 rabbit, skinned and paunched
yellow mustard
1 onion, peeled
1 carrot, peeled
1 leek, washed and trimmed
1 small clove garlic, peeled
half stick celery, washed
125 ml (¼ pint) dry white wine
1 Bouquet Garni (p. 22)
125 ml (¼ pint) water
salt and ground black pepper
1 sprig fresh tarragon *or* ½ teaspoon
   dried tarragon
1 piece pork rind, large enough to
   wrap completely around the rabbit
2 tablespoons double cream

Serves 4

Lapin aux Citrons
Rabbit with Lemon

1 kg (2 lb) cut rabbit joints
2 rashers lean bacon
40 g (1½ oz) butter
about 500 ml (1 pint) chicken *or* veal
    stock
8 very small onions, peeled
1 Bouquet Garni (p. 22)
salt and ground black pepper
2 lemons
(*optional*)
15 g (½ oz) butter to thicken
1 level tablespoon flour

Serves 4

Wash and dry the rabbit joints. Cut the bacon into matchstick strips. Melt the butter in a flameproof casserole and gently sauté the bacon and rabbit joints until the rabbit is golden all over. Add stock to just cover the rabbit, the onions, the bouquet garni, salt and pepper. Cover, and simmer very gently for 45 minutes, adding more boiling stock if it reduces to the extent that it no longer covers the rabbit.

Cut one of the lemons into fairly thin rounds. Lift the pieces of rabbit out of the pan, put the pieces of lemon in the bottom and put the rabbit back on top of them. Squeeze the juice of the other lemon into the pan, cover, and continue simmering gently until the rabbit is cooked, about another 45 minutes.

If you wish to thicken the sauce, cream the butter and flour together and beat it, little by little, into the sauce about 15 minutes before the rabbit is ready.

Check the seasoning and serve a slice of lemon with each piece of rabbit.

Selle de Chevreuil aux Marrons
Saddle of Venison with Chestnuts

*Always buy venison from a reputable game merchant who will have hung it according to the type of deer and prevailing weather conditions.

2 kg (4¼ lb) saddle of venison*
Basic Marinade (p. 28) made with
    white wine instead of red
50 g (2 oz) butter
1 kg (2 lb) chestnuts
1½ litres (about 3 pints) veal *or*
    chicken stock

Serves 8

Wash and dry the venison. Lay it in a large basin and pour the marinade over it. Leave it in a cold place for 2–3 days, turning it and spooning the marinade over it from time to time.

When ready to cook, prepare a hot oven preheated to 220°C, 425°F or Gas Mark 7. Remove the venison from the marinade, pat dry, and place skin side up in a roasting tin. Spread it with the butter and roast for 20 minutes in the hot oven. Lower the heat to 180°C, 350°F or Gas Mark 4 and continue cooking for another 1¼–1½ hours, basting frequently.

Meanwhile, spread the chestnuts on baking sheets and cook in the oven for 20 minutes, or until both outer and inner skins can be peeled off with a sharp knife. As they are skinned, put the chestnuts into a large shallow baking tin. When all are ready, bring the stock to the boil and pour over the chestnuts, adding boiling water if there is not enough stock to cover them completely. About 25 minutes before the venison is cooked, put the chestnuts in the oven beneath the meat. When they are tender, drain the chestnuts and use them to garnish the roast venison.

La Viande

Meat

The main difference between meat bought in France and meat bought in England is in the way it has been butchered. French butchers generally cut, bone and trim meat so that it is absolutely ready for cooking without further preparation or waste. This applies to the cheaper cuts such as brisket of beef, belly of pork and shoulder of lamb, as well as to the more expensive cuts. Very lean beef will be threaded through with thin stips of pure pork fat so that it does not dry out during the long slow cooking needed to tenderize it. Pork joints are usually skinned as well as boned, but the skin will be supplied for keeping the joint moist during cooking, or for using to enrich a slowly simmered wine stew. When veal is used in French recipes it should be, of course, the white milk-fed veal raised in Europe.

Bœuf à la Mode
Beef Braised in Wine

Ask the butcher to 'lard' the meat by running several thin strips of pork fat right through it.

Cut the belly pork into thin strips and heat gently in a heavy flameproof casserole until the fat is running freely. Put in the meat and brown lightly all over. Remove the meat and pork and pour away the fat. Chop all the vegetables roughly.

Line the bottom of the casserole with the pork rind, put in the beef, belly pork, calf's foot, vegetables and all the remaining ingredients. Add stock or water to reach half way up the meat. Cover the pan tightly and simmer over the lowest possible heat (use an asbestos or wire mat) for 4–5 hours. The meat will not come to harm if left even longer so long as it is turned at about half time.

Arrange the meat on a serving dish and keep hot. Strain the liquid into a saucepan, skim off the fat, and if necessary boil rapidly, uncovered, for a few minutes to reduce it. Check the seasoning. Pour a little of the sauce over the meat and serve the remainder separately.

1½ kg (3¼ lb) rolled silverside *or* topside
200 g (8 oz) sliced belly pork
2 onions, peeled
3 carrots, peeled
1 clove garlic, peeled
100 g (4 oz) pork rind
1 calf's foot, split in half
pinch nutmeg
1 clove
3 tablespoons brandy
125 ml (¼ pint) robust red wine
1 Bouquet Garni (p. 22)
salt and ground black pepper
stock *or* water

Serves 8–10

Pot-au-Feu en Gelée
Boiled Beef in Jelly

Measure the water into a large saucepan or stock-pot and put in the silverside, knuckle of veal, chicken necks and 1 level tablespoon salt. Bring slowly to the boil and simmer for 15 minutes, removing the scum as it rises. Roughly chop the carrots, leeks, turnips, celery and garlic, and add to the pan with the onion stuck with the cloves, and the bay leaf. Cover, and simmer for 3–3½ hours, or until the meat is *very* tender. Take the silverside and knuckle from the pan, remove the bones and sinews, and reserve the meat. Boil the liquid rapidly for 10 minutes, uncovered, then strain into a basin, check the seasoning, and leave in a cold place until set and jellied (if it does not set firmly return it to the saucepan with the bones and boil rapidly, uncovered, until further reduced). Remove the solidified fat from the face of the jelly, and then heat the jelly until just liquefied. Meanwhile, cut the meat into bite sized pieces and put into a deep china basin previously rinsed in cold water, and drained. If liked, add the pieces of carrot and turnip reserved from the cooking. Pour the cold, almost setting jelly over the meat, and leave in a cool place until set. Unmould, or serve from the basin.

3½ litres (6 pints) cold water
1 kg (2 lb) unsalted silverside
700 g (1½ lb) knuckle of veal (meat and bone)
200 g (8 oz) chicken necks
salt and ground black pepper
450 g (1 lb) carrots, peeled
3 leeks, well washed
3 small turnips, peeled
1 stick celery, washed
2–3 cloves garlic, peeled
1 onion, peeled
6 cloves
1 bay leaf

Serves 6–8

Bœuf Braisé des Bateliers d'Ampuis
Boatman's Braised Beef

1½ kg (3¼ lb) topside *or* top rump
250 ml (½ pint) white wine
2 tablespoons brandy
4 tablespoons olive oil
2 tablespoons wine vinegar
1 onion, peeled and chopped
1 sprig thyme
1 small bay leaf
3 large sprigs parsley
2 cloves
salt and ground black pepper
1 tablespoon oil
30 g (generous 1 oz) butter
4–6 onions, peeled and thinly sliced
½ bottle red wine
2 level tablespoons potato flour
   or cornflour
parsley butter (1 heaped tablespoon
   chopped parsley creamed with
   50 g (2 oz) butter and seasoning
   to taste)

Serves 8–10

Put the meat and all the ingredients down to and including the cloves into a deep china basin. Add a little salt and pepper and leave in a cold place to marinate for 3 days, turning the meat several times a day and spooning the marinade over it.

Take the meat out of the marinade and dry it. Heat the oil and butter in a large, heavy saucepan and gently fry the sliced onions until golden. Put in the meat and brown it all over. Strain the marinade over the meat and add the red wine. Cover the pan tightly and simmer very gently for 4 hours.

Take the meat out of the pan, carve it into thin slices, and overlap the slices on a large serving dish; keep warm. Meanwhile, boil the gravy rapidly, uncovered, until reduced a little. Blend the potato flour or cornflour smoothly with 2 tablespoons cold water, stir into the gravy and boil for another minute or two. Adjust the seasoning and pour the sauce over the meat. Immediately before serving, strew dabs of parsley butter over the meat.

Francine got this recipe from a small restaurant on the banks of the Rhône, the haunt of the boatmen who navigate this difficult river.

Bœuf à la Cuillère
Braised Beef

1½ kg (3¼ lb) rump steak in one thick
   round joint
a little olive oil
2 carrots, sliced
1 small onion, peeled
1 Bouquet Garni (p. 22)
salt and ground black pepper
500 ml (1 pint) beef *or* veal stock
50 g (2 oz) butter
450 g (1 lb) button mushrooms,
   washed
350 g (14 oz) can roulade de foie gras
   truffée
4 tablespoons jellied veal stock (p. 27)
   or medium-dry sherry

Serves 9 or 10

This is Francine's version of a traditional French recipe. Choose a deep flameproof casserole, just large enough to hold the meat comfortably, and film the bottom with oil. When very hot, brown the meat on all sides over a moderately high heat. This will take about 10 minutes. Add the carrots, onion, bouquet garni, some salt and pepper and the stock. Bring slowly to simmering point, then cover the pan tightly with kitchen foil and a lid. Simmer over the lowest possible heat for 3½–4 hours, or until very very tender.

Half an hour before serving, heat the butter in a heavy based pan and sauté the mushrooms gently, tossing frequently, for 10–15 minutes. Pass through the finest sieve of a vegetable mill or chop very finely. Mix the mushrooms and foie gras together thoroughly.

Remove the beef carefully from the cocotte and carve it across into equal sized slices, leaving each slice attached to its neighbour at the very bottom. Spread each slice with some of the mushroom mixture, press the joint together into its original shape, put on the serving dish and keep hot.

Remove the carrots, onion and bouquet garni from the casserole with a perforated spoon. Stir in the jellied stock or sherry and heat. The gravy should be concentrated, so, if necessary, boil quickly, uncovered, to reduce it. Pour the gravy over the meat.

Peas and young carrots go well with this dish and make a pretty garnish.

Ragoût de Bœuf Gitane
Gipsy Beef Stew

Cut the meat into strips the size of potato chips. Peel and slice the onions. Peel and dice the carrots and turnips. Heat the oil in a heavy-based saucepan and gently fry the onions until golden. Stir in the paprika. Put in the meat and stir over moderate heat until lightly sealed. Add the carrots and turnips and stir well, then add the marjoram or bay leaf, salt and pepper, and stock or water. Cover the pan tightly and simmer very gently for about 2 hours or until tender.

1 kg (generous 2 lb) topside of beef
2 medium onions
2 large carrots
2 small turnips
3 tablespoons oil
1 heaped teaspoon paprika
1 sprig marjoram *or* 1 bay leaf
salt and ground black pepper
250 ml ($\frac{1}{2}$ pint) stock *or* water

Serves 6

Bœuf à la Bourguignonne
Beef and Red Wine Stew

Trim the steak, cut into 2½ cm (1 inch) cubes and pat dry. Cut the pork slices into 1 cm ($\frac{1}{3}$-inch strips). Melt the dripping in a large flameproof casserole, and fry the pork strips and the button onions gently, stirring frequently, until the onions are golden. Remove the onions and reserve them. Add the chopped onion and the steak to the casserole and fry briskly, stirring frequently, until lightly browned. Sprinkle in the flour, and cook, stirring, for a minute or two. Stir in the wine, allow to bubble for a minute, then add the stock, tomato purée, garlic, bouquet garni, and salt and pepper. Bring to the boil, cover tightly, and simmer very gently on top of the cooker, or cook in a slow oven 150°C, 300°F or Gas Mark 2 for at least 2 hours. Check the seasoning, add the button onions, and continue cooking for another 30 minutes. Heat the butter and sauté the mushrooms for 5 minutes and add to the casserole just before serving.

1½ kg (3¼ lb) braising steak
200 g (8 oz) sliced salt belly pork
25 g (1 oz) dripping
200 g (8 oz) button onions, peeled
1 large onion, peeled and chopped
50 g (2 oz) flour
375 ml ($\frac{3}{4}$ pint) robust red wine
375 ml ($\frac{3}{4}$ pint) veal *or* beef stock
1 rounded tablespoon tomato purée
2 cloves garlic, crushed
large Bouquet Garni (p. 22)
salt and ground black pepper
40 g (1½ oz) butter
200 g (8 oz) button mushrooms, washed

Serves 8

Bœuf en Daube à la Marseillaise
Beef Stew Marseillaise

1 kg (generous 2 lb) chuck steak
250 ml (½ pint) robust red wine
2 tablespoons olive oil
ground black pepper
Bouquet Garni (p. 22)
1–2 cloves garlic, peeled
1 large onion
2 carrots
150 g (6 oz) unsmoked streaky bacon
300 g (12 oz) tomatoes
8 black olives
salt if necessary

Serves 4

Cut the meat into pieces about 5 cm (2 inches) square and 2½ cm (1 inch) thick. Put into a deep china bowl with the wine, oil, several grinds of black pepper, bouquet garni and garlic. Peel and slice the onion and carrots and add these to the marinade, stir well, cover, and leave in a cool place for at least 4 hours, or overnight if more convenient.

Cut the bacon into strips and cover the bottom of a casserole with half of it. Add the meat, vegetables and marinade. Peel, quarter and de-seed the tomatoes, add these to the casserole and then strew the rest of the bacon over the top. Cover tightly, and cook in the centre of a cool oven preheated to 150°C, 300°F or Gas Mark 2 for about 4 hours. Add the washed olives for the last 30 minutes. Before serving, discard the bouquet garni, skim off any surface fat, and adjust the seasoning, adding salt as necessary.

Serve from the casserole.

Rôti de Bœuf Jardinière
Roast Beef with Vegetables

1½ kg (3¼ lb) boned and rolled eye
  of sirloin
salt and ground black pepper
little olive oil
450 g (1 lb) small new potatoes
200 g (8 oz) small whole carrots
1 medium cauliflower
450 g (1 lb) French beans
450 g (1 lb) shelled peas
125 ml (¼ pint) red wine or dry white
  wine or beef stock

Serves 8

Preheat a hot oven to 220°C, 425°F or Gas Mark 7. Rub the meat with salt and pepper and brush all over with oil. Stand on a rack in a roasting tin and cook in the centre of the oven for 15 minutes. Lower the heat to 180°C, 350°F or Gas Mark 4 and continue cooking for 1–1¼ hours, or longer if you prefer well done beef. Meanwhile, prepare and cook the vegetables separately, according to kind, timing each carefully to avoid overcooking. Divide the cauliflower into flowerets.

To serve, carve the meat into slices and arrange overlapping each other down the centre of a large dish. Group the vegetables in piles all round the meat. Skim the surplus fat from the roasting tin, add the wine or stock and bring to the boil, stirring and scraping up the coagulated juices from the bottom of the tin. Boil for a minute, check the seasoning, and serve in a sauceboat.

Steaks au Poivre
Pepper Steaks

6 rump steaks, 150–175 g (6–7 oz)
  each
black peppercorns
white peppercorns
about 3 tablespoons olive oil
25 g (1 oz) clarified butter (p. 21)
salt
40 g (1½ oz) butter

Serves 6

There are several ways of serving these steaks but the cooking is the same for all. The variations are given at the end.

Depending on how peppery you want the steaks allow from ½–1 level teaspoon of mixed black and white coarsely ground pepper for each steak. Spread it over a plate and press first one side of the steak and then the other side into it. As each steak is peppered set it aside on a flat tray and sprinkle lightly with oil. Leave for at least half an hour to absorb the flavours.

To cook, heat the clarified butter and a tablespoon of oil in a heavy frying pan, and when sizzling put in the steaks and seal them quickly on each side. Lower the heat and cook to your liking, turning the steaks once more. Allow from 3–4 minutes each side for medium rare steaks, longer for well done. Take the steaks out of the pan, sprinkle with salt and keep hot. Put the unclarified butter into the frying pan and heat, scraping up all the juices from the base of the pan. Pour this over the steaks and serve as quickly as possible.

First variation
After taking the steaks out of the pan, pour in 125 ml ($\frac{1}{4}$-pint) white wine, boil briskly until well reduced, then off the heat stir in 50 g (2 oz) butter in small pieces. Pour over the steaks.

Second variation
After taking the steaks out of the pan, fry one finely chopped shallot until soft then add 125 ml ($\frac{1}{4}$-pint) robust red wine (preferably Burgundy) and boil briskly, stirring to scrape up the pan juices, until well reduced. Off the heat gradually stir in, 50 g (2 oz) butter. Pour over the steaks.

Third variation
Take the steaks out of the pan, pour in 4 tablespoons of brandy, light it and when the flame has gone out stir in 4 tablespoons cream. Pour over the steaks.

Chateaubriands Grande Severine
Fillet Steaks Grande Séverine

Trim the steaks if necessary and pat dry. Finely chop the shallots. Heat 40 g ($1\frac{1}{2}$ oz) of the butter in a heavy based pan and sauté the shallots *gently* until soft, about 5 minutes, then stir in the stock and keep hot. Heat the oil and remaining butter in a large frying pan, and when sizzling put in the steaks and seal them quickly on both sides. Lower the heat and cook the steaks to your liking, 3–4 minutes each side, or longer if you like them well done. Season with salt and pepper. Heat the brandy, light it and pour over the steaks, shaking the pan to distribute the flames evenly. When the flames have died down, arrange the steaks on a serving dish. Quickly add the shallots, cream, paprika and seasoning to taste to the pan and stir until hot. Pour over the steaks and serve at once.

6 thick steaks from the centre of the fillet
200 g (8 oz) shallots, peeled
75 g (3 oz) butter
125 ml ($\frac{1}{4}$ pint) jellied veal stock (p. 27)
1 tablespoon oil
salt and ground black pepper
6 tablespoons brandy
6 tablespoons double cream
1 teaspoon paprika pepper

Serves 6

Bifteck à l'Estouffade
Rump Steak Braised with Wine and Tomatoes

1 fat clove garlic
1 kg (generous 2 lb) thick slice rump
   steak
1 large onion
2 medium carrots
2 tablespoons oil
salt and ground black pepper
6 tablespoons dry white wine
2 tablespoons madeira *or* sherry
2 tablespoons brandy
450 g (1 lb) ripe tomatoes

Serves 6

Peel the garlic clove and cut in half. Dry the meat with kitchen paper and rub each side with the cut clove of garlic. Peel and slice the onion and carrots. Heat the oil in a wide, flameproof casserole and quickly brown the steak on each side. Remove from the pan and season with salt and pepper. Fry the onion and carrot in the same oil until beginning to colour, then replace the steak on top of the vegetables. Add the wines and brandy and allow to simmer for 1–2 minutes. Peel and quarter the tomatoes, spread over the meat and season lightly. Cover the casserole tightly and cook in the centre of a slow oven preheated to 150°C, 300°F or Gas Mark 2 for about 2 hours.

Serve from the casserole with creamed potatoes.

Tournedos aux Champignons
Tournedos with Mushrooms

*Tournedos are thick round tender rump or fillet steaks tied around with thin strips of pork fat.

450 g (1 lb) button mushrooms
50 g (2 oz) butter
50 g (2 oz) clarified butter (p. 21)
6 tournedos, about 150 g (6 oz) each*
salt and ground black pepper
6 rounds fried bread
5 tablespoons medium dry Madeira
   or sherry
3 tablespoons jellied veal stock (p. 27)
1 level teaspoon potato flour *or*
   cornflour

Serves 6

Wash the mushrooms and pat dry. Melt the ordinary butter and sauté the mushrooms gently for 10 minutes, tossing frequently. Heat the clarified butter in a heavy frying pan, and when hot put in the tournedos and seal quickly on both sides. Lower the heat, dust the top of the tournedos with salt and pepper, and put the mushrooms in the pan with them. Cook for 2–3 minutes, then turn the tournedos, and dust with salt and pepper. Cook a further 2–3 minutes, or longer if you like steak well done.

Put each tournedos on a piece of fried bread, arrange on a serving dish, set a few mushrooms on top of each and pile the rest in the centre of the dish. Keep hot.

Add the sherry and stock to the frying pan and bring to the boil, stirring to scrape up the juices from the bottom of the pan. Blend the flour to a smooth paste with 1 tablespoon water, stir into the pan and simmer for a minute or two, stirring. Check the seasoning and serve this sauce separately.

Bifteck Haché à la Lyonnaise
Minced Lyonnaise Beef Cakes

3 tablespoons olive oil
100 g (4 oz) finely chopped onion
700 g (1½ lb) lean minced beef
salt and ground black pepper
1 large egg, beaten
a little flour
125 ml (¼ pint) red *or* white wine
25 g (1 oz) softened butter

Serves 4

Heat 1½ tablespoons of the oil in a small frying pan and fry the onion for about 10 minutes, until soft but not browned. Turn into a bowl, add the beef, seasoning to taste, and the beaten egg, mix very thoroughly. Form into eight small round cakes about 1¼ cm (½-inch) thick. Cover, and refrigerate.

When ready to cook, lightly coat the beef cakes with flour. Heat the remaining oil in a large frying pan and, when hot, fry the cakes for about 3 minutes each side. Transfer to a serving dish and keep hot. Pour the wine into the same frying pan and boil rapidly for a minute or two, stirring up the co-agulated juices from the bottom of the pan, until well reduced and syrupy. Take off the heat and stir in the butter, then spoon a little sauce over each meat cake.

Queue de Bœuf à la Mode
Marinated Oxtail

Start making this dish the day before it is required. Ask the butcher to chop the oxtail into equal sized pieces and to split the foot.

Put the pieces of oxtail into a china basin, add the wine, brandy, nutmeg, salt and pepper and leave in a cool place to marinate for 24 hours, stirring occasionally.

Take the pieces of oxtail out of the marinade and dry them. Heat 40 g (1½ oz) of the butter in a heavy based saucepan, and when hot add the bacon, onions and carrots. Brown lightly over moderate heat, stirring frequently. Add the oxtail and brown lightly. Add the bouquet garni, foot, marinade and stock or water. Cover the pan tightly and simmer over the lowest possible heat for 3 hours. Pour off all the liquid and leave overnight in a cool place so that the fat can solidify on the surface.

Half an hour before serving, heat the remaining butter in a heavy based saucepan and cook the pickling onions very gently, covered, shaking the pan frequently. Discard the foot and bouquet garni from the oxtail. Remove the fat from the stock and pour the liquid over the oxtail. Bring gently to simmering point and simmer until the onions are cooked.

Arrange the pieces of oxtail in a deep serving dish. Add the onions and their butter to the gravy in the pan, check the seasoning, and stir and boil for a few minutes. Pour the gravy and vegetables over the meat.

1 large or 2 small oxtails
1 calf's or pig's foot
½ bottle robust red wine
4 tablespoons brandy
pinch nutmeg
salt and ground black pepper
75 g (3 oz) butter
4 rashers unsmoked streaky bacon, diced
3 onions, peeled and sliced
3 large carrots, peeled and sliced
1 Bouquet Garni (p. 22)
125 ml (¼ pint) stock or water
200 g (8 oz) small pickling onions, peeled

Serves 4

Blanquette de Veau Francine
Francine's Creamed Veal

1¼ kg (2½–3 lb) boneless shoulder
  veal
125 g (5 oz) butter
salt and ground black pepper
1 large carrot, peeled and quartered
1 large onion, peeled and quartered
1 Bouquet Garni (p. 22)
1 litre (1¾ pints) veal stock *or* water
200 g (8 oz) can button onions
450 g (1 lb) button mushrooms,
  washed
40 g (1½ oz) flour
2 egg yolks
3 tablespoons double cream
1–2 tablespoons lemon juice

Serves 8

Cut the meat into 2½ cm (1 inch) cubes. Heat 40 g (1½ oz) of the butter in a heavy based saucepan and sauté the meat over moderate heat for 15 minutes, stirring frequently, until pale gold all over. Season with salt and pepper, add the carrot, onion, bouquet garni and stock or water. Cover, and simmer gently for 1 hour, or until tender. Drain off the stock, measure, and if necessary make up to 750 ml (1½ pints) with water. Discard the vegetables and bouquet.

Meanwhile, drain and dry the canned onions and sauté gently in 25 g (1 oz) butter until golden. In another pan, sauté the mushrooms in 25 g (1 oz) butter for 5–10 minutes, tossing frequently.

Thicken the sauce as follows. Melt remaining butter in a large, flameproof serving casserole. Add the flour and cook, stirring, for a minute. Add the measured stock all at once and whisk briskly until boiling, then simmer for several minutes. Blend the egg yolks and cream together, stir in a little of the hot liquid, then return to the casserole, whisking all the time. Take off the heat and add lemon juice to taste, adjust the seasoning and replace the meat. Heat through gently, but do not allow to boil.

Serve garnished with the button onions and mushrooms.

Roulade de Veau Fourée
Stuffed Rolled Veal

*Ask the butcher to bone and flatten a breast of veal wide enough for rolling and stuffing. Use the bones for making the stock.

1½ kg (3¼ lb) boned breast of veal,
  weight after boning*
veal stock (p. 27)
150 g (6 oz) cooked ham
100 g (4 oz) mushrooms, washed
200 g (8 oz) pure pork sausage meat
2 eggs
40½ g (10 z) can truffle peelings
  (optional)
75 g (3 oz) butter
2 shallots, peeled and chopped
1 clove garlic, peeled and crushed
salt and ground black pepper
2 tablespoons double cream

Serves 9 or 10

Lay the veal flat, skin side down. Fold the two long edges together, overlapping by 1½ cm (½-inch) and sew them together with needle and thread thus forming a tube for stuffing. Stand the tube upright on a circle of oiled kitchen foil.

Make the stuffing. Finely chop the ham and mushrooms and add to the sausage meat with the beaten eggs and truffle peelings, if used. Melt 40 g (1½ oz) of the butter and fry the shallots and garlic for a minute, then stir into the stuffing and mix all together thoroughly. Season if necessary. Put the stuffing into the veal 'tube', pressing it well down so that no gaps are left. Cover with another circle of kitchen foil and tie this, and the lower circle, firmly in position to hold the stuffing in place. Preheat a very moderate oven 170°C, 325°F or Gas Mark 3 and heat the remaining butter in an oval cocotte. When hot, put in the veal and baste it. Cook in the centre of the oven for 2½–3 hours, turning it once.

To serve, arrange the veal on a serving dish and remove the string and foil; keep hot. Pour 125 ml ($\frac{1}{4}$-pint) of stock into the cocotte and boil briskly for a minute or so, stirring. Check the seasoning. Take off the heat, stir in the cream and pour the sauce over the veal.

This dish can be eaten either hot, or cold with mayonnaise.

Poitrine de Veau Farcie
Stuffed Breast of Veal

Melt 30 g (generous 1 oz) of the butter and sauté the mushrooms for a minute or two. Skin the kidney, cut it lengthways in half and remove the fat and core sinew. Mince or finely chop the kidney, bacon, tongue, onion, mushrooms and herbs. Put into a basin, add the spice, egg yolks and salt and pepper to taste, then mix thoroughly. Lay the veal flat, skin side down, spread with the stuffing and roll up into a sausage shape. Tie securely in several places. Heat the remaining butter and the oil in an oval shaped cocotte, and brown the veal roll lightly all over. Add the stock, cover the cocotte tightly and cook in a very moderate oven 170°C, 325°F or Gas Mark 3 for 2–2$\frac{1}{2}$ hours or until tender, turning once. Place the veal on a serving dish and remove the string.

Serve with the well reduced and seasoned gravy poured over.

75 g (3 oz) butter
200 g (8 oz) mushrooms, washed
1 veal kidney
3 rashers unsmoked streaky bacon
200 g (8 oz) cooked tongue
1 medium onion, peeled
1 teaspoon fresh mixed herbs
 or $\frac{1}{4}$ teaspoon dried
1 pinch mixed spice
2 egg yolks
salt and ground black pepper
1$\frac{1}{2}$ kg (3$\frac{1}{4}$ lb) boned breast of veal*
2 tablespoons oil
250 ml ($\frac{1}{2}$ pint) veal stock (p. 122)

Serves 9 or 10

Veau aux Oranges
Veal with Oranges

Finely chop two of the carrots and cut the others into very fine slices (a mandoline cutter is very useful for this purpose). Heat the oil and half of the butter in a heavy casserole and brown the veal and onions in it. When everything is well coloured heat the brandy, light it and pour over the meat. When the flames have died down, add half of the wine and some salt and pepper. Cover the pan and cook in the centre of a very moderate oven preheated to 170°C, 325°F or Gas Mark 3 for 1 hour. Squeeze the juice from three of the oranges, pour it over the veal, cover, and continue cooking for another 30 minutes or until the meat is tender.

Meanwhile, as soon as the veal is in the oven, cut the pork into large matchstick pieces and put into a heavy saucepan with the remaining butter. Cook gently until the pork fat is running freely, then add the sliced carrots, pepper and very little salt. Cover the pan tightly and cook over the lowest possible heat (use an asbestos or wire mat if necessary). If the carrots show signs of browning add the smallest possible quantity of water. When tender, remove from the heat and keep warm. Peel and

1 kg (2 lb) carrots, peeled
1 tablespoon oil
75 g (3 oz) butter
1$\frac{1}{4}$ kg (2–3$\frac{1}{2}$ lb) boneless veal roasting
 joint
4 smallish onions, peeled
6 tablespoons brandy
250 ml ($\frac{1}{2}$ pint) dry white wine
salt and ground black pepper
5 oranges
1 thin slice pickled belly pork

Serves 6–8

slice the remaining oranges.

When the meat is cooked, arrange it, with the vegetables from the pan, on a serving dish. Surround with the sliced carrots and edge the dish with the orange slices. Pour the remaining wine into the casserole, and simmer, stirring, over low heat for several minutes. Check the seasoning and serve separately.

Veau à la Provençal
Veal with Olives

50 g (2 oz) butter
1¼ kg (2½–3 lb) boneless veal roasting joint
2 tablespoons olive oil
8 small onions, peeled and sliced
3 carrots, peeled and sliced
1 sprig thyme
1 bay leaf
salt and ground black pepper
100 g (4 oz) green pitted olives
100 g (4 oz) black pitted olives
100 g (4 oz) button mushrooms, washed
125 ml (¼ pint) veal or chicken stock
2 tablespoons port
125 ml (¼ pint) double cream
2 tablespoons chopped parsley

Serves 6–8

Preheat a hot oven to 200°C, 400°F or Gas Mark 6. Put the butter into a flameproof casserole and put into the oven to heat. Brush the veal all over with the oil, then put into the melted butter with any remaining oil. Surround with the onions and carrots and add the thyme, bay leaf and a sprinkling of salt and pepper. Turn the meat until lightly browned on all sides. Lower the heat to 170°C, 325°F or Gas Mark 3 and cook slowly, covered, for about 1½ hours in all, or until the veal is tender. After 1 hour add the olives, mushrooms, stock and port.

When the meat is ready, transfer it to a serving dish. Lift out all the vegetables with a perforated spoon and arrange round the meat; keep hot. Put the casserole on top of the cooker and whisk in the cream; heat slowly but do not allow to boil. Stir in the parsley, adjust the seasoning, and serve separately.

Tendrons de Veau
Tendrons of Veal

*Tendrons of veal are thick slices cut from the centre of the breast

6 tendrons of veal, about 125 g (5 oz) each*
a little seasoned flour
25 g (1 oz) butter
1 tablespoon oil
200 g (8 oz) onions, peeled and chopped
450 g (1 lb) tomatoes, peeled
1 Bouquet Garni (p. 22)
1 strip lemon rind
1 level tablespoon tomato purée
250 ml (½ pint) dry white wine
salt and ground black pepper
2 tablespoons chopped parsley

Serves 6

Dip the tendrons of veal into the seasoned flour, pressing it on well. Heat the butter and oil in a wide, heavy based saucepan and lightly brown the tendrons on each side; remove. Add the onions and sauté gently for 5 minutes. Meanwhile, halve the tomatoes, remove the seeds and chop the flesh. Add the chopped tomatoes to the onions and cook gently for 3 minutes. Add the bouquet garni, lemon rind, tomato purée, wine and salt and pepper to taste. Replace the tendrons, and spoon the sauce over them. Cover the pan and simmer for 1½ hours or until very tender. Arrange the tendrons on a serving dish. Discard the bouquet garni and lemon rind from the sauce, stir in the parsley and simmer for several minutes. Check the seasoning and pour over the veal.

Veau Thonné
Veal with Tuna

Cut the meat into 2½ cm (1 inch) cubes. Heat the butter and oil in a flameproof casserole and sauté the meat until lightly coloured all over. Chop the onion, shallot and garlic, and add to the meat with the bouquet garni, wine and salt and pepper to taste. Allow to simmer, uncovered, for 15 minutes, then cover the pan and continue simmering gently for 1 hour. Drain the oil from the tuna fish. Chop the fish and add to the veal with the slices of lemon. Cover, and continue simmering for 15 minutes, or until the meat is tender. Serve hot in the casserole.

700 g (1½ lb) boned knuckle of veal
25 g (1 oz) butter
1 tablespoon oil
1 large onion, peeled
1 shallot, peeled
1 small clove garlic, peeled
1 Bouquet Garni (see p. 22)
250 ml (½ pint) dry white wine
salt and ground black pepper
198 g (7 oz) can tuna fish in oil
4 slices lemon

Serves 4

Grenadins de Veau Francine
Francine's Grenadins of Veal

*In France, grenadins are *thick* miniature steaks cut across the grain from a piece of the leg corresponding to the roll of the silverside in beef. They are encircled with barding fat, and sometimes larded as well.

Heat the butter in a flameproof casserole and when hot, brown the grenadins quickly on each side. Lower the heat, cover the pan and cook *very gently* for 15 minutes. Add the wine, salt and pepper. Cover the casserole, transfer to a preheated very moderate oven (170°C, 325°F or Gas Mark 3) and cook for 5 minutes. Add the brandy, cover, and continue cooking for another 10 minutes, or a little longer if you like veal very well cooked.

50 g (2 oz) clarified butter
6 veal grenadins*
125 ml (¼ pint) dry white wine
salt and pepper
1 tablespoon brandy

Serves 3

Côtelettes de Veau à la Foyot
Veal Cutlets Foyot

Season the veal cutlets lightly with salt and pepper. Heat 30 g (generous 1 oz) of the butter and the oil in a frying pan and fry the *chopped* onion gently until soft, but not browned. Spread on top of the veal cutlets. Melt another 50 g (2 oz) butter in the same pan. Mix the white breadcrumbs and cheese together, sprinkle half evenly over the cutlets on top of the onions, and press down firmly. Sprinkle with a few drops of the melted butter, then with the remaining breadcrumb and cheese mixture. Sprinkle again with melted butter, then cover with the browned crumbs.

Melt another 30 g (generous 1 oz) butter and fry the *sliced* onions slowly until soft and pale gold. Spread them over the bottom of a flameproof dish, just large enough to hold the cutlets in a single layer. Pour in the wine and stock around the edge of the dish so that it does not come above the level of the

4 thick veal cutlets
salt and ground black pepper
125 g (5 oz) butter
1 tablespoon oil
4 heaped tablespoons very finely chopped onion
4 heaped tablespoons white breadcrumbs
4 heaped tablespoons grated cheese
4 level tablespoons browned breadcrumbs
2 large onions, peeled and sliced
4 tablespoons dry white wine
4 tablespoons meat stock

Serves 4

meat. Sprinkle the cutlets with a little more melted butter.

Put the dish over a low heat until the liquid just begins to simmer, then transfer to a moderate oven preheated to 180°C, 350°F or Gas Mark 4 and cook for about 45 minutes. Sprinkle with a little more butter once or twice during the cooking, and if the liquid reduces too much add a little more wine or stock. Serve hot, with the pan juices poured around, but not over, the cutlets.

Alouettes sans Tête
Stuffed Veal Escallops

6 thin escallops of veal, 50–75 g (2–3 oz) each
3 shallots, peeled
200 g (8 oz) mushrooms, washed
75 g (3 oz) butter
2 tablespoons chopped parsley, mixed if possible with fresh chervil and tarragon
100 g (4 oz) pure pork sausage meat
1 egg
salt and ground black pepper
6 small thin slices cooked ham
6 slices barding fat (p. 21)
1 large onion, sliced
1 large carrot, sliced
1 Bouquet Garni (p. 22)
6 tablespoons white wine
250 ml (½ pint) veal *or* chicken stock

Serves 4–6

If necessary, place the escallops between greaseproof paper and beat until very thin. Make the stuffing as follows. Mince or finely chop the shallots and mushrooms. Melt 30 g (generous 1 oz) of the butter in a heavy saucepan and gently sauté the shallots and mushrooms until the onion is soft. Add the herbs and sausage meat and mix thoroughly over gentle heat. Cool the stuffing for a few minutes, then stir in the egg and seasoning to taste.

Lay a slice of ham on each escallop, spread the stuffing on top, roll up the escallops and tuck in the ends. Tie the barding fat around them.

Melt the remaining butter in a sauté pan and fry the sliced onion gently until pale gold. Put in the veal rolls and brown lightly, then add the carrot, bouquet garni, seasoning and wine. Simmer for about 5 minutes, add the stock, then cover, and transfer to a very moderate oven preheated to 170°C, 325°F or Gas Mark 3. Cook for about 45–60 minutes, basting occasionally.

To serve, discard the string and barding fat, arrange the rolls on a serving dish and keep hot. Add a tablespoon or so of cold water to the casserole, bring to the boil, stirring, and if necessary boil hard for a few minutes to reduce the quantity and concentrate the flavour. Strain the sauce over the veal rolls.

Escalopes de Veau Joséphine
Veal Escallops Josephine

6 thin escallops of veal
1 teaspoon mixed chopped basil and sage *or* ½ teaspoon dried
6 thin slices Parma ham
a little seasoned flour
65 g (2½ oz) butter
1 tablespoon oil
1 tablespoon very finely chopped shallot
8 tablespoons dry white vermouth
salt and ground black pepper

Serves 6

Lay the escallops flat and scatter a pinch or two of herbs over each. Roll them up, wrap a slice of ham around each and secure with a cocktail stick. Roll in seasoned flour and press the coating on firmly.

When ready to cook, melt 40 g (1½ oz) of the butter and the oil in a frying pan and sauté the rolled escallops gently for 8–10 minutes, turning them from time to time so that they cook and colour evenly all over. Remove them from the pan and keep hot on a serving dish. Stir the shallot into the frying pan and cook for a minute or two until slightly golden. Add the vermouth, bring quickly to the boil, then take off the cooker and stir in the remaining butter. Check the seasoning and pour over the escallops. Serve at once.

Nids d'Hirondelles
Swallows' Nests

Place the escallops between greaseproof paper and beat each until large enough and thin enough to wrap completely around an egg. Season with pepper. Remove any rind or bone from the bacon rashers and lay two, flat, on each escallop. Place a hard-boiled egg in the centre of each and roll up, folding the ends in neatly. Secure by winding cotton thread around several times. Heat the butter and oil in a heavy based pan, and when hot lightly brown the veal rolls all over. Dust with a little pepper, add the wine and water, cover the pan tightly and simmer *very gently* for about 45 minutes, turning once or twice to cook evenly. Should the liquid evaporate too much, add a little more water.

When the rolls are cooked, remove the cotton, and serve the rolls cut in half so that the yolk of egg is seen surrounded by the white of egg and then by the veal.

6 long shaped escallops of veal
ground black pepper
12 thin rashers lean unsmoked bacon
6 hard-boiled eggs
25 g (1 oz) butter
1 tablespoon oil
4 tablespoons dry white wine
4 tablespoons water

Serves 6

Cœurs de Veau Farcis
Stuffed Veal Hearts

Soak the hearts in cold salted water for 30 minutes. Cut out the tubes and membranes and make a large cavity in each heart. Rinse in cold water and then dry them. Make the stuffing. Finely chop the shallots and mushrooms. Heat 40 g (1½ oz) of the butter in a frying pan, and fry the shallots and mushrooms gently for 5 minutes, stirring frequently. Take off the heat and add the sausage meat, nutmeg, and seasoning if necessary; mix thoroughly. Press the stuffing well down into the heart cavities, and keep in place with a piece of oiled double greaseproof paper tied in position. Heat the remaining butter in a heavy based, flameproof casserole and brown the hearts all over. Cover tightly, and cook in a very moderate oven preheated to 170°C, 325°F or Gas Mark 3 for 1½–2 hours. To serve, remove the paper and string and divide the hearts in half. If liked, add a scant 125 ml (¼-pint) water to the casserole and boil rapidly for a minute or two, stirring and scraping the coagulated juices from the bottom of the casserole. Check the seasoning and pour a little of the sauce over each portion of heart.

2 small veal hearts, about 450 g (1 lb) each
4 shallots, peeled
200 g (8 oz) mushrooms, washed
75 g (3 oz) butter
200 g (8 oz) pure pork sausage meat
pinch nutmeg
salt and ground black pepper

Serves 4–6

Rognons de Veau à la Crème, Sauce Moutarde
Veal Kidneys with Mustard Cream Sauce

4 veal kidneys, about 150 g (6 oz) each
40 g (1½ oz) butter
1 tablespoon oil
salt and ground black pepper
4–5 heaped teaspoons French mustard
175 ml (⅓ pint) double cream

Serves 4

Soak the kidneys in cold salted water for 30 minutes. Skin them, cut them lengthways about half through, and remove any fat or sinews without destroying the shape of the kidneys. Pat dry. Heat the butter and oil in a heavy saucepan, and when really hot put in the kidneys and brown them lightly all over. Sprinkle with salt and pepper, lower the heat and sauté for about 15 minutes, turning from time to time. Meanwhile whisk the mustard into the cream. When the kidneys are done, take them out of the pan and keep hot. Pour the cream into the saucepan and whisk vigorously to combine it with the kidney juices. When hot check the seasoning and pour the sauce over.

Rognons Sautés Madère
Veal Kidneys in Madeira Sauce

3–4 veal kidneys, about 150 g (6 oz) each
40 g (1½ oz) butter
1 level tablespoon flour
125 ml (¼ pint) veal *or* chicken stock
3 tablespoons Madeira
salt and ground black pepper
1 teaspoon lemon juice
1 tablespoon chopped parsley

Serves 3 or 4

Skin the kidneys and cut into 1 cm (⅓-inch) slices. Heat the butter in a large frying pan and fry the kidney slices fairly briskly for 3–4 minutes, turning to brown lightly on each side. Remove from the pan, cover and keep warm. Sprinkle the flour into the pan, stir and cook for a minute or two until pale brown in colour. Stir in the stock, Madeira and seasoning to taste, and simmer gently for 5 minutes. Replace the kidney slices and their juices, add the lemon juice and heat for several minutes without boiling. Serve immediately sprinkled with chopped parsley.

Quenelles de Veau Alsacienne
Liver Quenelles Alsatian Style

300 g (12 oz) calf's *or* lamb's liver
50 g (2 oz) cooked lean ham
1 bridge roll *or* 1 slice bread
a little milk
1 egg
1 rounded tablespoon flour
1 rounded tablespoon semolina
1 small onion, very finely chopped
1 tablespoon chopped parsley
salt and ground black pepper to taste

Serves 4

Mince the liver and ham. Soak the bridge roll or bread in a little milk, then squeeze out surplus milk and add the soft crumbs to the liver. Add all the other ingredients and mix and mash thoroughly with a fork.

Bring a deep saucepan of lightly salted water to the boil.

Shape the quenelles by taking a rounded tablespoon of the mixture and sliding it into the simmering water with the help of another tablespoon, keeping the form as near egg shaped as possible. Don't overcrowd the pan. When the quenelles rise to the surface, in 5–7 minutes' time, they are cooked. Lift out with a perforated spoon, and keep warm until all are ready.

This is the classic recipe, but Francine liked the quenelles even better if, after they were cooked, they were drained and then lightly browned on all sides in butter.

Beckenoff ou Potée à la Boulangère
Beckenoff or Baker's Casserole

This dish must be prepared the day before it is to be cooked.

Cut all the meat into 2½ cm (1 inch) cubes. Put it into a deep basin with half of the onions, the garlic, bay leaf, cloves, carrots, some salt and pepper and the wine. Leave overnight in a cool place, turning the meat over occasionally during the evening. About 3 hours before the dish is required, peel the potatoes and cut into slices a little thicker than a 10p piece. Spread half of the potatoes over the bottom of a wide earthenware casserole and dust with salt and pepper. Put in the meat and all the ingredients and wine from the marinade, add the remaining chopped onion and cover with the rest of the potato slices. Cover the casserole tightly with buttered cooking foil and a lid, and cook in the centre of a slow oven preheated to 170°C, 325°F or Gas Mark 3 for 2½–3 hours or until very tender.

Do not open the casserole until it is on the table so that the full flavour hasn't a second to evaporate. Beckenoff is the Alsatian name for this dish, but it is well known by its other name all over France. It used to be the custom to take this dish to the baker's to be cooked in the oven after the bread baking was finished.

450 g (1 lb) lean, boneless shoulder of lamb
450 g (1 lb) lean, boneless braising beef
450 g (1 lb) lean, boneless shoulder of pork
2 large onions, peeled and chopped
1 or 2 cloves garlic, peeled
1 bay leaf
2 cloves
2 large carrots, peeled and sliced
salt and ground black pepper
250 ml (½ pint) dry white wine
1 kg (2 lb) potatoes
a little butter

Serves 8–10

Epaule de Mouton au Riz
Shoulder of Mutton with Rice

Ask the butcher to bone, roll and tie the meat. Heat the butter and oil in a heavy casserole, and when hot, brown the meat on all sides. Heat the brandy, light it, and pour flaming over the joint. Add salt, pepper and stock, cover the pan, and cook in the centre of a moderately slow oven preheated to 170°C, 325°F or Gas Mark 3 for about 2½ hours. Meanwhile, cook the rice in boiling salted water for 15 minutes, then drain, run cold water through it, and drain again thoroughly. About 15 minutes before serving, put the rice into the casserole with the meat to finish cooking and become impregnated with the savoury stock. Remove the meat from the casserole, drain the rice, and serve together.

1 shoulder of mutton *or* lamb, about 1¼ kg (3 lb)
25 g (1 oz) butter
1 tablespoon oil
6 tablespoons brandy
salt and ground black pepper
1 litre (1¾ pints) meat stock
200 g (8 oz) rice

Serves 8

Epaule d' Agneau Farcie
Stuffed Shoulder of Lamb

1¼ kg (2½–3 lb) shoulder of lamb
200 g (8 oz) cooked ham
100 g (4 oz) carrots, peeled
100 g (4 oz) mushrooms, washed
1 large onion, peeled
bunch fresh parsley
200 g (8 oz) pork sausage meat
75 g (3 oz) butter
2 level tablespoons tomato purée
salt and ground black pepper
2 tablespoons brandy
4 tablespoons medium sherry
125 ml (¼ pint) stock *or* water

Serves 6

Ask the butcher to bone but not roll the meat. Mince the ham, carrots, mushrooms, onion and fresh parsley, then mix thoroughly with the sausage meat. Heat 25 g (1 oz) of the butter in a frying pan and sauté the mixture for 2–3 minutes. Stir in the tomato purée and leave to cool. Lay the meat flat and skin side down, season with salt and pepper, spread the stuffing over it, and roll up. Tie securely in several places. Heat the remaining butter in a heavy braising pan and brown the meat lightly all over. Heat the brandy, light it and pour flaming over the meat. When the flames have gone out, add the sherry and stock or water. Cover the pan tightly and simmer very gently for 2½ hours. Remove the string and arrange the meat on a serving dish. Skim off any fat from the cooking liquid, adjust the seasoning and pour into a sauce boat.

Selle d' Agneau Gitane
Gipsy Saddle of Lamb

*A saddle of lamb consists of the two loins joined in the centre. In France, butchers cut a saddle with short shanks making a compact joint.

1 saddle of lean lamb, about 2 kg
  (4½ lb)*
olive oil
about 3 tablespoons fresh paprika
salt and ground black pepper
100 g (4 oz) canned anchovy fillets
50 g (2 oz) butter
1 clove garlic, peeled and crushed
8–10 small tomatoes, peeled
2 tablespoons double cream
2 tablespoons brandy
pinch grated nutmeg

Serves 8–10

Brush the meat all over with oil, then rub the paprika into it. Stand the joint in a baking tin and put into a preheated very hot oven 220°C, 425°F or Gas Mark 7 for 10 minutes. Season with salt and pepper. Lower the heat to 180°C, 350°F or Gas Mark 4 for the rest of the cooking time, 1½–2 hours in all, depending on how well cooked you like lamb. Put the anchovy fillets, butter and garlic into a mortar or strong basin and pound together to a cream. After the joint has been cooking for 50 minutes, spread it generously all over with the anchovy cream, and continue cooking. Twenty minutes before serving time, put the tomatoes into a casserole, sprinkle with 2 tablespoons of oil and a little salt and pepper. Cover, and cook below the joint. When cooked, remove the lamb to a serving dish, surround with the tomatoes and keep hot. Stir the cream, brandy and nutmeg into the juices in the roasting tin, bring to the boil and pour into the gravy boat.

1 saddle of lamb, about 2 kg (4½ lb)*
salt and ground black pepper
200 g (8 oz) butter
4 good stalks fresh tarragon
1 handful tarragon leaves, finely
  chopped
8–10 slices of French bread

Serves 8–10

Selle d' Agneau au Beurre d'Estragon
Saddle of Lamb with Tarragon Butter

Rub the meat with salt and pepper on both sides. Preheat a moderate oven 180°C, 350°F or Gas Mark 4 and melt 50 g (2 oz) of the butter in a baking tin. Put in the saddle, baste it immediately, and lay two stalks of tarragon in the tin on either side of the meat. Cook in the centre of the oven, basting frequently, for 1½–2 hours, depending on how well done you like lamb.

Cream the remaining butter with the chopped tarragon and a little salt and pepper; put aside to chill. Just before the lamb is cooked, toast the slices of bread and spread with the tarragon butter. Remove the lamb to a serving dish and keep hot. Remove the stalks of tarragon from the roasting tin, add 125 ml (¼-pint) cold water, stir until boiling, and then simmer for several minutes. Adjust the seasoning and pour into a sauceboat. Spread the remaining tarragon butter on top of the saddle so that the melting butter will scent the meat with tarragon. Arrange the pieces of toast around the meat, and serve immediately.

Les Côtes Jumelles aux Aromates
Twin Chops with Herbs

*Two chops cut right across the loin so they remain joined in the centre

Trim excess fat from the chops, and scrape 1 cm (⅓-inch) of the thin end of the bone clean. Warm the oil, add the mixed dried herbs and bay leaf, cover, and leave to infuse for at least 30 minutes. Strain through a fine sieve. Cut out a small tube shaped wedge from the stalk end of each tomato, press a slice of garlic and sprig of rosemary into each, add salt and pepper and a few drops of the herb-flavoured oil. Put them in a baking tin, sprinkle with more oil, and bake in a moderate oven preheated to 180°C, 350°F or Gas Mark 4 for about 15 minutes. While they are cooking, wipe the chops well with the remaining oil and put a sage leaf on each. Put more sage in the grill pan. Heat the grill and grill the chops, turning them once, for about 8 minutes in all. The hot fat falling on the sage gives them a beautiful flavour. Serve with the tomatoes arranged on the same dish.

6 pairs double loin chops*
6 tablespoons olive oil
1 level tablespoon mixed dried
  rosemary, sage, thyme and
  marjoram
1 bay leaf
12 medium sized firm tomatoes
3–4 cloves garlic, peeled and sliced
12 small sprigs fresh or dried
  rosemary
salt and ground black pepper
fresh sage leaves, if available

Serves 6

Hachis à la Niçoise
Mince Nice Style

Mince the meat. Soak the bread in a little milk with salt and pepper. Squeeze out surplus milk and mash the bread with the meat. Add the herbs and eggs, mix thoroughly, and season to taste. Slice the tomatoes in rounds. Butter a deep ovenproof dish, put in alternate layers of tomatoes, meat and macaroni, beginning and ending with tomatoes. Sprinkle with breadcrumbs and dot with the rest of the butter. Cook towards the top of a preheated hot oven 200°C, 400°F or Gas Mark 6 for 30 minutes.

200 g (8 oz) cold cooked mutton *or*
  lamb
1 thick slice bread, without crusts
a little milk
salt and ground black pepper
½ tablespoon mixed chopped fresh
  herbs – parsley, chives, chervil and
  tarragon, as available
2 small eggs, beaten
700 g (1½ lb) ripe tomatoes, peeled
25 g (1 oz) butter
200 g (8 oz) cooked macaroni (75 g
  (3 oz) raw)
some dried breadcrumbs

Serves 3 or 4

12 lean lamb cutlets
50 g (2 oz) butter
1 kg (generous 2 lb) ripe tomatoes,
  peeled
6 large onions, peeled and sliced
6 cloves garlic, peeled and sliced
100 g (4 oz) de-seeded or seedless
  raisins
2 level tablespoons tomato purée
3 large cooking apples, peeled, cored
  and quartered
salt and ground black pepper

Serves 6

Sauté d'Agneau
Lamb and Tomato Stew

Remove any surplus fat from the cutlets. Heat the butter in a large flameproof casserole and brown the cutlets on both sides. Quarter and de-seed the tomatoes, and add to the meat with the onions, garlic, raisins, tomato purée, apples and seasoning to taste. Cover the pan tightly and simmer very gently for 1–1½ hours, stirring occasionally. Check the seasoning and serve from the casserole.

50 g (2 oz) dried haricot beans
1 kg (generous 2 lb) boneless
  shoulder of lamb
1 tablespoon oil
25 g (1 oz) butter
2 level tablespoons flour
salt and ground black pepper
1 Bouquet Garni (p. 22)
300 g (12 oz) ripe tomatoes, peeled
  and quartered
200 (8 oz) turnips, peeled
  and quartered
200 g (8 oz) carrots, peeled and
  quartered
450 g (1 lb) small new potatoes
6 small onions, peeled
200 g (8 oz) shelled peas

Serves 5 or 6

Navarin Printanier
Spring Lamb Stew

Soak the beans overnight in cold water. All the other vegetables should be very young and tender. Cut the meat into 2½ cm 1 inch) cubes. Heat the oil and butter in a large, heavy braising pan (large enough to hold all the other ingredients) and fry the meat until lightly browned. Sprinkle in the flour and cook, stirring, until pale brown, then stir in just enough water to cover the meat. Add seasoning to taste and stir until boiling. Add the bouquet garni, tomatoes and drained beans (the latter will cook to a pulp and make a creamier gravy). Cover the pan tightly, and simmer for 1 hour. Add the turnips, carrots, potatoes and onions, pushing them under the liquid. If necessary, add a little more water just to cover them. Simmer for another hour then add the peas and continue simmering until they are cooked (10 minutes for frozen peas but 15–20 minutes if fresh). Adjust the seasoning and serve from the casserole.

350 g (12–14 oz) lamb's or calf's liver
2 aubergines
salt
oil for frying
2 large onions, peeled and sliced
a little seasoned flour
450 g (1 lb) tomatoes, skinned and
  sliced
1 clove garlic

Serves 4

Foie à la Basquaise
Liver in Basque Style

Cut the liver into thin slices, wash and dry. Cut the aubergines into 1 cm (⅓-inch) thick slices, sprinkle with salt and leave in a colander to drain for an hour or so. Pat dry with kitchen paper. Heat 3–4 tablespoons oil in a large frying pan and fry the aubergine slices a few at a time, until cooked through and golden, adding more oil to the pan as necessary. When cooked, arrange them on a large serving dish and keep warm. Fry the onions gently in the same pan for 15 minutes, or until soft and golden; then remove and scatter over the aubergines. Dip the slices of liver in the seasoned flour and then fry quickly for about 2 minutes each side. Arrange on top of the onions. Finally fry the tomatoes and garlic. Arrange these around the edge of the dish and sprinkle with the parsley. Serve very hot with plain boiled potatoes or crusty French bread.

Brochettes Ecossaises
Kidneys and Bacon on a Skewer

Remove the fat and skin from the kidneys and cut them in halves. Remove the bacon rinds and cut the rashers into squares—you will need twenty-eight pieces in all. Fry the pieces of bacon in a large frying pan, stirring frequently, until the fat begins to run freely and the bacon is cooked; remove from the pan. Add the butter to the bacon fat and when hot fry the pieces of kidney in it until lightly browned, then lower the heat and cook gently for 5 minutes in all. Reserve pan juices. Spear alternate pieces of bacon and kidney on four metal skewers, beginning and finishing with bacon. Push into the centre of the skewers, leaving the ends free. Select a saucepan just large enough for the skewers to rest across the top, and put the whisky into it. Heat the whisky, light it, and quickly rest the skewers across the top of the pan; turn them round and round as long as the whisky is alight. Remove and keep hot. Put the water into the frying pan in which the kidneys were cooked, stir and scrape the bottom while bringing to the boil. Tip these buttery juices into the whisky pan, add the mustard, cummin and pepper, bring just to the boil, then remove from the heat and stir in the cream. Serve the brochettes dusted with chives and hand the sauce separately.

12 lambs' kidneys
200 g (8 oz) unsmoked, streaky bacon
  rashers
50 g (2 oz) butter
4 tablespoons whisky
1 tablespoon water
1 level teaspoon made English
  mustard
1 level teaspoon crushed cummin
ground black pepper
3 tablespoons double cream
chopped fresh chives to garnish

Serves 4

Rognons Pannés
Breadcrumbed Kidneys in Wine Sauce

Remove the fat and skin from the kidneys and cut them across in thin slices. Dip the kidney slices first in the seasoned flour, then in beaten egg and finally in the breadcrumbs. Heat the butter and oil in a large shallow frying pan and fry the kidney slices on both sides for about 3 minutes in all. Take them out and keep hot. Stir the 1 level tablespoon flour into the pan and when perfectly smooth stir in, little by little, first the wine and then the sherry. Simmer for a few minutes, stirring all the time, then add the parsley and seasoning to taste. Pour the sauce over the kidneys and serve very hot.

12 lambs' kidneys
a little seasoned flour
2 small eggs, well beaten
dried white breadcrumbs
50 g (2 oz) butter
1 tablespoon oil
1 level tablespoon flour
6 tablespoons white wine
2 tablespoons medium sherry
1 tablespoon chopped, fresh parsley
salt and ground black pepper

Serves 4

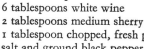

Côtelettes à la Charcuterie
Butcher's Pork Chops

3 lean pork chops
salt
30 g (generous 1 oz) butter
2 level tablespoons flour
2 level teaspoons tomato purée
250 ml (½ pint) hot water
6 gherkins
6 pickled onions
1 level tablespoon capers
2 teaspoons wine vinegar
ground black pepper

Serves 3

Cut off any rind, then plunge the chops into boiling salted water and leave for 5 minutes to make them tender.

Meanwhile, melt the butter in a sauté pan, add the flour and cook, stirring, over gentle heat for a minute or two. Stir in the tomato purée and the hot water, then bring to the boil, stirring all the time. Chop the gherkins and pickled onions finely, and add to the sauce with the capers and seasoning to taste. Drain the chops, put them into the sauce, cover the pan and simmer very gently for about 30 minutes. Just before serving stir in the vinegar and check the seasoning.

Côtelettes du Porc aux Aromates
Pork Chops with Herbs

For each person:
1 pork chop
a little oil
ground black pepper
sprays of sage, thyme and bay (with sage predominating)
salt
a little chopped fresh *or* dried sage

Trim the chop, removing the rind and surplus fat. Brush with oil and sprinkle with pepper. Put the herb sprays in the bottom of the grill pan and place the chop on the grid. Preheat the grill, then cook the chop under maximum heat for a minute or so until sealed on both sides. Lower the heat and cook gently allowing 5–7 minutes each side in all. As it cooks the hot fat will fall on the herbs and their scent will penetrate the meat. When cooked, season with salt, sprinkle with chopped or dried sage and serve very hot.

Côtes de Porc, Pays d'Auge
Normandy Pork Chops

4 pork chops
25 g (1 oz) butter
2 large cooking apples
2–3 tablespoons Calvados
2 tablespoons water
salt and ground black pepper

Serves 4

Trim the chops, removing the rind and surplus fat. Heat the butter in a sauté pan and very gently brown the chops on both sides. Peel, core and roughly chop the apples and spread them over the bottom of a wide ovenproof casserole. Arrange the chops on the apples, add the Calvados, water and seasoning. Cover the casserole and cook in the centre of a preheated moderately slow oven 170°C, 325°F or Gas Mark 3 for 30–40 minutes. Serve from the casserole.

Côtelettes de Porc Niçoises
Pork Chops Nice Style

4 canned anchovy fillets
50 g (2 oz) butter
1 heaped tablespoon finely chopped mixed sage, basil and tarragon
4 pork chops
ground black pepper

Serves 4

Put the anchovies, butter and herbs into a mortar or strong basin and pound to a cream. Set aside in a cool place to harden. Trim the chops, removing the rind and surplus fat. Season them with pepper. Preheat the grill to maximum then grill the chops for a minute or so to seal each side. Lower the heat to moderate and cook steadily until cooked through, allowing from 5–7 minutes each side in all, depending on thickness.

Spread a little anchovy and herb butter on each chop and serve immediately.

Carré du Porc Maréchal
Loin of Pork with Ham and Mushrooms

Ask the butcher to remove the rind from the pork and to roll and tie the joint securely. Preheat a very hot oven to 220°C, 425°F or Gas Mark 7, and melt 25 g (1 oz) of the butter in a roasting tin. When hot, roll the pork over and over in the butter and cook for 5 minutes each side in the hot oven. Lower the heat to 180°C, 350°F or Gas Mark 4 and cook for 1½ hours, basting from time to time.

Melt the remaining butter in a sauté pan and fry the mushrooms gently for 10 minutes or until their liquid has evaporated. Chop the mushrooms and ham finely and then mix them into the Béchamel Sauce with seasonings of salt, pepper and nutmeg.

When the meat is cooked, carve it down in slices, but without detaching them at the base of the joint. Spread about 1 tablespoon of the mushroom mixture between each slice. Press the joint back into shape and put it on an ovenproof serving dish. Spread a thin coating of the mushroom mixture over the top, and spoon the remainder along each side of the meat. Scatter the cheese over it. Return to a very hot oven 220°C, 425°F or Gas Mark 7 for 10–15 minutes for the cheese to melt and colour lightly.

1¼ kg (2½–3 lb) boned and rolled loin of pork
50 g (2 oz) butter
450 g (1 lb) button mushrooms, washed
200 g (8 oz) cooked ham
500 ml (1 pint) coating Béchamel Sauce (p. 22)
salt and ground black pepper
a little grated nutmeg
100 g (4 oz) grated Parmesan cheese

Serves 8 or 9

Porc à la Mode des Vosges
Loin of Pork with Carrots and Wine

Ask the butcher to remove the rind and bone and roll the pork. Preheat a very hot oven to 220°C, 425°F or Gas Mark 7. Season the meat well, place on a rack in a baking tin, fat side downwards, and cook for 5 minutes. Turn fat side up and cook for another 5 minutes. Lower the heat to 180°C, 350°F or Gas Mark 4 and continue cooking, allowing 1 hour 20 minutes per kg (2 lb) (35 minutes per 450 g (1 lb) weight). Cut the carrots into 1 cm (⅓-inch) thick slices. About 45 minutes before the pork is ready, put the carrots into a heavy saucepan with the butter, wine and some salt and pepper; simmer very gently until tender, about 15–20 minutes. Drain off the cooking liquid and pour over the pork; and from now on baste the meat frequently. When the pork is cooked, arrange it on a serving dish and surround with the carrots. Pour the juices from the

1½ kg (3¼ lb) loin of pork
salt and ground black pepper
1 kg (2 lb) young carrots, scraped
25 g (1 oz) butter
250 ml (½ pint) dry white wine

Serves 8

baking tin very slowly into a very cold basin, and spoon off the surplus fat as it rises. Return the gravy to the baking tin and bring to the boil, stirring and scraping the coagulated juices from the bottom of the tin. Boil rapidly for a few minutes to reduce the gravy, then adjust the seasoning. Pour a little gravy over the pork, and serve the rest separately.

Sauté de Porc à la Cannes
Casserole of Pork Cannes Style

1 kg (2 lb) lean boneless pork (hand of pork *or* boned shoulder)
1½ tablespoons olive oil
2 shallots, peeled and chopped
1 medium onion, peeled and chopped
1 clove garlic, peeled and chopped
1 sprig thyme
1 small bay leaf
½ teaspoon paprika
1 pinch mixed spice
salt and ground black pepper
1½ level tablespoons flour
about ½ bottle dry white wine
150 g (6 oz) shelled peas
75 g (3 oz) green *or* black olives
1 sweet pepper, de-seeded and sliced

Serves 5 or 6

Cut the pork into 2½ cm (1 inch) cubes. Heat the oil in a large flameproof casserole, and when hot brown the meat quickly, stirring frequently. Add the shallots, onion, garlic, thyme, bay leaf, paprika, spice, salt and pepper. Lower the heat, and sauté stirring, for several minutes. Add the flour and stir until it colours slightly, then stir in enough wine just to cover the meat. Continue stirring until the sauce boils and thickens slightly. Cover the pan tightly and simmer very gently for 1 hour. Skim off any surface fat, then stir in the peas, olives and green pepper, cover, and continue simmering for another 30 minutes. Check the seasoning, remove the herbs, and serve from the casserole.

Sauté de Porc Mireille
Casserole of Pork Mireille

550 g (1¼ lb) aubergines
salt
1 kg (generous 2 lb) boneless pork (boned hand *or* shoulder)
about 5 tablespoons oil
1 kg (generous 2 lb) ripe tomatoes
2 medium onions, peeled and chopped
1 clove garlic, peeled and chopped
1 teaspoon paprika
pinch powdered saffron
ground black pepper
a little seasoned flour
oil for deep frying
1 sweet red pepper
1 sweet green pepper

Serves 6

Peel the aubergines, cut into 2 cm (¾-inch) cubes, and put into a colander, sprinkling each layer lightly with salt. Leave to drain for 1 hour. Cut the pork into 2½ cm (1 inch) cubes. Heat 1 tablespoon of oil in a large, flameproof casserole and brown the meat quickly all over. Peel and quarter half of the tomatoes and add to the casserole with half of the chopped onions and garlic. Add the paprika, saffron, salt and pepper and stir well. Cover the casserole tightly and simmer very gently for 2 hours. After 1½ hours prepare the rest of the ingredients. Heat a deep pan of frying oil to 190°C or 375°F. Dry the cubes of aubergine, toss them in seasoned flour, and fry in the hot fat until lightly browned, for about 5 minutes; drain and keep hot. Halve the remaining tomatoes. Heat 2 tablespoons oil in a wide pan, add the remaining onion and garlic, and fry gently for a few minutes. Put the tomatoes into the pan, cut side down, and cook until lightly coloured, then turn over and continue cooking until you can remove the skins easily. Cover, and leave on one side. Grill the peppers under brisk heat, turning frequently until the skin has blackened and blistered on all sides. Then wash off the skin, cut the peppers lengthways into 2½ cm (1 inch) wide strips, and remove all the seeds. Fry gently in 2 tablespoons of hot oil until tender, about 10–15 minutes, cover the pan, and leave on one side. About 5 minutes before serving, gently reheat the tomatoes and peppers. Stir the aubergine, tomatoes and some of the pepper strips into the casserole and check the seasoning. Turn the stew into a deep serving dish and garnish with the remaining strips of pepper.

Sauté de Porc Francine
Francine's Stewed Pork

Cut the pork into 2½ cm (1 inch) cubes. Heat the lard in a strong, flame-proof casserole and sauté the onions slowly until golden. Stir in the pork, cover the pan tightly and cook over *very low* heat for 15 minutes, stirring occasionally. Add the tomatoes, tomato purée, bouquet garni, paprika, wine, stock and salt and pepper. Stir well then cover the pan tightly and simmer over very low heat for 2½ hours. If the tomatoes are really ripe, no additional liquid should be needed, but if the pork seems to be getting dry, add a little more wine, stock or water. Adjust the seasoning, and serve from the casserole.

Beef can be used in this recipe instead of pork.

1 kg (2¼ lb) any lean boneless cut of pork (e.g. hand of pork *or* lean shoulder)
25 g (1 oz) lard
200 g (8 oz) onions, peeled and chopped
450 g (1 lb) ripe tomatoes, skinned and quartered
2 level tablespoons tomato purée
1 Bouquet Garni (p. 22)
1 teaspoon paprika
125 ml (¼ pint) white wine
125 ml (¼ pint) stock
salt and ground black pepper

Serves 6

Rôti de Porc Forestière
Foresters' Roast Pork

Put the pork into a deep china bowl and pour the marinade over it. Leave in a cool place for 24 hours, turning and basting the pork several times.

Lift the meat from the marinade and pat dry with kitchen paper. Heat 25 g (1 oz) of the butter in a flameproof casserole and brown the meat lightly all over. Transfer to the centre of a moderate oven preheated to 180°C, 350°F or Gas Mark 4. Cook, uncovered, allowing 45 minutes per 450 g (1 lb) weight, and basting occasionally.

Ten minutes before the meat is ready, heat the remaining 50g (2 oz) butter in a large sauté pan, add the mushrooms, lemon juice and a little salt and pepper, and cook gently, covered, shaking the pan frequently.

When the pork is cooked remove it to a serving dish, surround with the mushrooms and keep hot. Pour off the excess fat from the casserole, strain the marinade into the remaining juices and boil fast, uncovered, for several minutes until well reduced. Check the seasoning and pour into a sauceboat.

French beans and tender young carrots make a good garnish for this dish.

1½ kg (3¼ lb) boned leg of pork
Basic Marinade (p. 28)
75 g (3 oz) butter
1 kg (2 lb) fresh mushrooms, washed
1 tablespoon lemon juice
salt and ground black pepper

Serves 8 or 9

Porc Flambé
Blazed Roast Pork

1½ kg (3¼ lb) middle cut leg of pork
a little olive oil
2 or 3 cloves garlic, peeled
1 rounded teaspoon paprika
salt and ground black pepper
1 rounded tablespoon mixed chopped
    fresh thyme and sage *or* 1 level
    tablespoon dried thyme and sage
1 kg (2 lb) tiny new potatoes, scraped
4 tablespoons brandy *or* whisky

Serves 8 or 9

Ask the butcher to remove the pork rind. Brush the joint all over with the oil. Cut the garlic cloves in half and rub over the meat, then dust with the paprika, salt and pepper and the herbs. Leave in a cool place for at least one hour.

Stand the pork on a grid in a roasting tin and cook in the centre of a very hot oven preheated to 230°C, 450°F or Gas Mark 8 for 5 minutes, then lower the heat to moderate 180°C, 350°F or Gas Mark 4 and cook for 45 minutes per 450 g (1 lb) weight. One hour before the meat is ready, put the potatoes into the roasting tin beneath the meat, turning them over once to coat with fat.

When cooked, remove the pork to a flameproof serving dish and surround with the drained potatoes. Heat the spirit in a small saucepan, carry the dish and pan to the table, pour the spirit over the meat and light it.

Porc aux Pruneaux
Pork with Prunes

16 large prunes
250 ml (½ pint) robust red wine
    (*or* medium-dry white wine)
4 thin slices pork from the top leg,
    150 g (5–6 oz) each
1 tablespoon oil
25 g (1 oz) butter
salt and ground black pepper
1 tablespoon redcurrant jelly
125 ml (¼ pint) double cream

Serves 4

Soak the prunes overnight in the wine. Next day, simmer them in the wine for 20–30 minutes, until tender. Trim any rind from the pork. Heat the oil and butter in a wide sauté pan and fry the slices of pork quickly on each side to seal them. Lower the heat, season with salt and pepper and cook very, very gently (using an asbestos or wire mat if necessary), covered, for 25–30 minutes or until tender. Arrange the pork down the centre of a serving dish and keep hot.

Strain the wine from the prunes into the sauté pan. Stir and scrape the juices from the bottom of the pan and then boil rapidly until reduced by half. Add the jelly, and when dissolved, stir in the cream. Cook gently, stirring, until the sauce thickens. Pour over the pork and arrange the prunes all round the dish.

Porc au Chou Rouge
Pork with Red Cabbage

1 kg (generous 2 lb) red cabbage
50 g (2 oz) pork dripping *or* butter
300 g (12 oz) cooking apples, peeled
    and sliced
300 g (12 oz) onions, peeled and
    sliced
salt and ground black pepper
1 clove garlic, peeled and crushed
large pinch ground cloves
125 ml (¼ pint) red wine
125 ml (¼ pint) stock *or* water
1 kg (generous 2 lb) boneless
    shoulder pork

Serves 6

Cut the cabbage into quarters and then into thin slices. Melt the fat in a large heavy saucepan, then add the cabbage and all the other ingredients except the pork. Cover tightly, and cook over the lowest possible heat for at least 2 hours, stirring occasionally. If the cabbage appears to be getting dry, add a little more stock or water. Alternatively, bring to the boil on top of the cooker and then transfer to a slow oven preheated to 150°C, 300°F or Gas Mark 2 and cook for 2–2½ hours, or until tender. Cut the pork into 2½ cm (1 inch) cubes and add to the cabbage, stirring it in well. Continue cooking slowly for another hour or until both the pork and cabbage are tender. Check the seasoning and serve hot.

Porc au Riz
Pork with Rice

Cut the meat into 2½ cm (1 inch) cubes. Chop the onions. Melt 40 g (1½ oz) of the butter in a heavy saucepan and cook the onions gently until almost translucent and just beginning to colour. Add the pork and fry until lightly browned, then season with salt and pepper. Add the flour and stir until well blended, then add the tomato purée, parsley and mushrooms (quartered if large). Cover the pan tightly and cook over the lowest possible heat, using an asbestos or wire mat, for 15 minutes. Add the cummin, bay leaf and thyme, and enough water just to cover the meat. Cover the pan tightly, and simmer very gently for 1½ hours, adding a little more water only if necessary. Half an hour before serving, cook the rice in plenty of fast boiling salted water until just tender, which will take from 15–20 minutes depending on variety. Drain, return to the pan with the remaining butter, cover with a clean cloth and the lid, and keep warm. Remove the herbs from the pork, check the seasoning and serve surrounded by the rice.

700 g (1½ lb) boneless thick end of belly of pork
2 large onions, peeled
65 g (2½ oz) butter
salt and ground black pepper
1 level tablespoon flour
2 level tablespoons tomato purée
1 tablespoon chopped parsley
100 g (4 oz) mushrooms, washed
pinch cummin
1 bay leaf
1 sprig thyme
200 g (8 oz) long grain rice

Serves 4

Pieds de Contrebandiers
Smuggler's Trotters

Wash the trotters thoroughly in cold salted water. Put them into the court bouillon, bring to the boil and simmer gently, covered for about 35 minutes, or until the flesh leaves the bones easily. Remove the trotters, and when cool enough to handle, slit them lengthways and remove all the bones. Season the insides with pepper. Reshape each trotter as well as possible and place on a piece of caul. Slice the truffles, if used, and arrange some on top of each trotter. Roll up firmly in the caul, then roll in the breadcrumbs and press the coating on firmly. Arrange the trotters in a single layer, side by side, in an oven-proof dish and dot with 25 g (1 oz) of the butter. Cook towards the top of a hot oven preheated to 200°C, 400°F or Gas Mark 6 until heated through and lightly browned, 25–30 minutes. Meanwhile, turn the chestnut purée into a saucepan and heat with the remaining butter and a little salt and pepper. Serve the trotters and chestnut purée together on the same dish.

6–8 pig's trotters
salt and ground black pepper
1½ litres (2½ pints) cold Court Bouillon (p. 28)
6–8 pieces pig's caul
50 g (2 oz) can truffles (optional)
some fine white breadcrumbs
50 g (2 oz) butter
450 g (1 lb) can unsweetened chestnut purée

Serves 6–8

Du Petit Salé aux Lentilles
Boiled Bacon with Lentils

1 kg (2 lb) collar bacon joint
25 g (1 oz) lard
200 g (8 oz) pickling onions, peeled
ground black pepper
2 sticks celery
3 carrots
450 g (1 lb) large brown lentils
Bouquet Garni (p. 22)
2 cloves garlic, peeled and crushed

Serves 6

Cover the bacon joint with cold water, bring slowly to the boil, then drain, rinse and dry. Melt the lard in a deep flame-proof casserole, put in the bacon joint, onions and a seasoning of pepper, but no salt. Wash the celery and cut into 2½ cm (1 inch) pieces. Scrape and halve the carrots. When the onions begin to colour, add the lentils, celery, carrots, bouquet garni and garlic. Cover with cold water, bring to the boil, and simmer very gently, tightly covered, for about 2 hours or until the lentils are cooked. Take out the bacon, cut into slices, arrange on a serving dish and keep warm. Strain the vegetables and lentils, and arrange them around the meat, discarding the bouquet garni.

Tranches de Jambon à la Crème
Ham Slices in Cream Sauce

4 slices cooked ham, 1 cm (⅜ inch) thick
25 g (1 oz) butter
2 teaspoons oil
1 heaped tablespoon finely chopped shallots
1 level tablespoon flour
125 ml (¼ pint) ham *or* chicken stock
4 tablespoons Madeira
1 teaspoon tomato purée
ground black pepper
125 ml (¼ pint) double cream
1 kg (2¼ lb) spinach, cooked and squeezed dry

Serves 4

Trim any excess fat from the ham. Heat the butter and oil in a large frying pan and fry the ham slices until lightly browned on each side; remove and keep warm. Add the shallots, stir and fry gently for a minute or two, then stir in the flour and cook, stirring, for another minute or so. Heat the stock and Madeira and then stir smoothly into the shallots and flour. Add the tomato purée and pepper, bring to the boil and simmer gently for a minute, then stir in the cream and continue cooking gently, stirring, for several minutes until the sauce is of a light coating consistency. Check the seasoning, put in the ham slices and reheat gently. Serve on a bed of chopped spinach.

Les Pâtés et les Terrines

Pâtés and Terrines

With the exception of the Herb Terrine (p. 145) Francine recommended that all these pâtés be served cold, also that they would keep for at least a week in a refrigerator and are therefore a great standby.

Presumably Francine intended them to be served from the terrine as no mention is made of cooling them under weights or of turning them out. In the absence of a traditional earthenware terrine use a soufflé dish, casserole or pie dish of a suitable size. The cooking time will vary a little according to the depth of the mixture, deep dishes needing longer. Generally speaking the pâté is cooked when the mixture has shrunk from the sides of the dish and the fatty juices are colourless.

Pâtés are at their best if allowed to 'mature' for 2–3 days in the refrigerator before being eaten. Serve with either freshly made hot toast or crusty French bread, and unsalted butter. Robust red wines go well with pâtés.

Francine used the traditional French method for game and chicken pâtés of stripping the flesh off the bird in its raw state. This is rather a messy job for the uninitiated (although the carcase makes excellent broth) and one which is easier to handle if the bird is half cooked before stripping.

Terrine de Volaille
Chicken Terrine

Skin the chicken, and with a sharp knife take off the breast and wing meat and cut into thick matchstick pieces. Put these to marinate in the brandy with salt, pepper and cayenne for at least an hour, turning the pieces of chicken over from time to time. Take off the rest of the chicken meat and chop it finely (or mince it coarsely) with the fresh and pickled pork, the shallots and garlic. Add the eggs, the truffle peelings and their juice (if used), the brandy marinade, the spice and salt and pepper to taste. Mix together very thoroughly. Line a generous 1 litre (2 pint) capacity terrine with barding fat, put in alternate layers of minced meats and marinated chicken, ending with minced meats. Top with thin strips of barding fat, cover with kitchen foil and a lid, and stand in a baking tin with hot water to reach half way up the dish. Cook in the centre of a moderate oven preheated to 170°C, 325°F or Gas Mark 3 for about 1¾–2 hours. Set aside to become cold.

1 chicken, weighing about 1½ kg
(3¼ lb)
4 tablespoons brandy
salt and pepper
pinch cayenne
200 g (8 oz) fresh belly pork*
200 g (8 oz) pickled belly pork*
3 shallots, peeled
1 or 2 cloves garlic, peeled
2 eggs, beaten
15 g (½ oz) can truffle peelings
(optional)
pinch mixed spice
200 g (8 oz) barding fat (p. 21)

Serves 7 or 8
*Weighed without skin and bone

Terrine des Foies de Volaille de Claude
Chicken Liver Terrine

Wash the livers and discard any membranes or discoloured pieces. Put into a basin with the port and leave to marinate for at least an hour. Finely chop the bacon, ham and truffles if used, and add to the sausage meat. Stir in the port from the marinade and the white wine. Crush the peppercorns and add a little to the mixture with a little salt. Taste, and continue to add pepper until the seasoning is to your liking. Chop about a third of the livers, add them to the mixture, and mix again thoroughly. Line a 1¼ litre (2–2¼ pint) terrine with thin strips of barding fat, put in alternate layers of the mixture and the whole or halved livers, ending with a layer of mixture. Cover this with barding fat, then cover the terrine with kitchen foil and a lid. Stand in a baking tin with hot water to reach half way up the terrine and cook in the centre of a moderate oven preheated to 180°C, 350°F or Gas Mark 4 for about 1½ hours.

450 g (1 lb) chicken *or* mixed poultry
livers
4 tablespoons port
100 g (4 oz) unsmoked streaky bacon
100 g (4 oz) Parma *or* Bayonne ham*
15 g (½ oz) can truffles (optional)
300 g (12 oz) pork sausage meat
(p. 24)
4 tablespoons dry white wine
2 or 3 black peppercorns
salt
200 g (8 oz) barding fat (p. 21)

Serves 8
*Specially cured ham which is eaten
raw. Lean raw gammon is the
nearest substitute

Terrine de Canard à l'Orange
Duck and Orange Terrine

1 young wild duck, about 700 g
  1½ lb)
4 tablespoons brandy
200 g (8 oz) fresh belly pork*
200 g (8 oz) veal*
1 shallot, peeled
1 orange
2 small eggs, beaten
pinch powdered thyme
pinch powdered savory
salt and ground black pepper
200 g (8 oz) barding fat (p. 21)
thin slices of orange to garnish

Serves 5 or 6
*Weighed without skin and bone

Carve the breast meat off the bird into small thin fillets and put them to marinate in the brandy for 2–3 hours. Finely chop the rest of the duck meat together with the pork, veal and shallot, or pass all through the coarse blades of a mincer. Peel the orange rind very thinly (a potato peeler does this job admirably) and cut it into very fine matchsticks. Mix this with the chopped meat, add the eggs, brandy of the marinade, herbs and generous seasonings of salt and pepper. Line a 625 ml 1¼ pint) capacity terrine with thin slices of barding fat, put in alternate layers of chopped meat and fillets, finishing with chopped meat. Cover with strips of barding fat. Seal the terrine with kitchen foil, and set in a baking tin half filled with hot water. Cook in the centre of a moderate oven pre-heated to 170°C, 325°F or Gas Mark 3 for about 1 hour. When cold, open the terrine, and before serving garnish the top with thin slices of orange.

Terrine de Faisan aux Olives
Pheasant and Olive Terrine

1 young pheasant, weighing 1 kg
  (about 2¼ lb)
4 tablespoons brandy
200 g (8 oz) veal
200 g (8 oz) fresh belly pork
50 g (2 oz) pitted green olives
1 shallot, peeled
2 small eggs, beaten
pinch mixed dried herbs
salt and ground black pepper
200 g (8 oz) barding fat (p. 21)

Serves 7 or 8

Slice the pheasant breast meat thinly and put to marinate in the brandy for 2–3 hours. Cut the rest of the meat off the bird and finely chop it together with the veal, pork, most of the olives and the shallot (or pass all through the coarse blades of a mincer). Add the eggs, herbs, brandy of the marinade, salt and pepper; mix very thoroughly. Line a 625 ml (1¼ pint) capacity terrine with thin slices of barding fat, put in alternate layers of minced meat and pheasant slices, ending with minced meat. Halve the remaining olives and arrange them over the top and cover with slices of barding fat. Seal the terrine with kitchen foil and set in a baking tin half filled with hot water. Cook in the centre of a moderate oven preheated to 170°C, 325°F or Gas Mark 3 for about 1 hour, or 1½ hours if using a casserole pheasant. Serve cold.

Terrine de Bécasses aux Truffes
Truffled Woodcock Terrine

4 fresh woodcock, oven-ready (see
  p. 108)
25 g (1 oz) can truffles (optional)
6 tablespoons brandy
200 g (8 oz) chicken or calf's liver
salt and ground black pepper
2 eggs, beaten
200 g (8 oz) barding fat (p. 21)

Serves 4–6

Remove and set aside the offal from each woodcock. Cut the breast meat off the birds in neat slices, put into a bowl with the truffles and brandy and leave to marinate for 2–3 hours. Take the remaining meat off the birds and chop it finely with all the offal and the chicken or calf's liver. Add salt and pepper, and then the brandy of the marinade. Cut the truffles into fine slices, set aside 3 or 4 and mix the others into the chopped meat. Add the eggs and mix thoroughly again. Line a 1¼ litre (2 pint) capacity terrine with thin slices of barding fat, put in alternate layers of chopped meats and slices, ending with chopped meats. Put the reserved truffle slices on top then cover with more barding fat. Seal the terrine with kitchen foil, and set in a baking tin half filled with hot water. Cook in the centre of a moderate oven preheated to 170°C, 325°F or Gas Mark 3 for about 1 hour. Serve cold.

Terrine de Lapin de Garenne
Wild Rabbit Terrine

Slice the meat from the rabbit legs and back into small thin strips, put them into a bowl with the brandy, salt and pepper and leave for 2–3 hours, turning the meat over in the marinade fairly often. Peel the shallots, garlic and onion. Take the rest of the meat off the rabbit and mince it with the rabbit's liver, the shallots, garlic, onion, belly pork and thyme. Soak the bread in the milk, squeeze out surplus milk and mash the bread into the mince. Add spice, cayenne, salt and pepper, beaten egg and the marinade drained from the rabbit; mix very thoroughly. Line a 1¼ litre (2 pint) terrine with thin strips of barding fat, put in alternate layers of mince and sliced meat, ending with a layer of mince. Cover with slices of barding fat and lay the bay leaf on top. Cover the terrine with kitchen foil and the lid, and set in a baking tin with hot water to reach half way up the dish. Cook in the centre of a moderate oven preheated to 170°C, 325°F or Gas Mark 3 for about 1½ hours. Serve very cold.

1½ kg (3¼ lb) rabbit*
5 tablespoons brandy
salt and ground black pepper
2 shallots
1 clove garlic
1 small onion
200 g (8 oz) fresh belly pork
1 sprig thyme
1 slice bread
a little milk
pinch mixed spice
pinch cayenne
1 egg, beaten
200 g (8 oz) barding fat (p. 21)
1 small bay leaf

Serves 6
*Weight after skinning and cleaning

Terrine aux Aromates
Herb Terrine

Wash and prepare the spinach, and cook in a small amount of boiling salted water for 5 minutes. Drain thoroughly and then squeeze in your hands to press out any remaining water. Chop it roughly. Finely chop (or coarsely mince) the ham, bacon, onion, garlic, bay leaf and fresh herbs. Add to the spinach with the egg, pork sausage meat, and salt and pepper. Mix all these ingredients together very thoroughly. Line a 1¼ litre (2–2¼ pint) terrine with thin strips of barding fat, pack in the spinach mixture and cover with more slices of barding fat. Seal the terrine with kitchen foil and stand in a baking tin with hot water to reach half way up the sides. Cook in the centre of a very moderate oven 170°C, 325°F or Gas Mark 3 for about 1 hour. This terrine may be eaten hot or cold.

450 g (1 lb) spinach
salt
100 g (4 oz) cooked ham
100 g (4 oz) unsmoked streaky bacon
1 medium onion, peeled
1 clove garlic, peeled
1 small bay leaf
2–3 tablespoons mixed fresh herbs
  (parsley, basil, savory, rosemary)
1 egg, beaten
450 g (1 lb) pork sausage meat (p. 24)
ground black pepper
200 g (8 oz) barding fat (p. 21)

Serves 6

Terrine de Veau et Porc
Veal and Pork Terrine

1 medium onion
1 shallot
1 clove garlic
1 medium carrot
450 g (1 lb) leg of pork*
300 g (12 oz) veal*
1 tablespoon chopped parsley
2 tablespoons olive oil
pinch mixed spice
pinch ground nutmeg
salt and ground black pepper
¼ bottle Sauternes *or* sweet white
    wine
15 g (½ oz) truffle peelings (optional)
300 g (12 oz) pork sausage meat
    (p. 24)
200 g (8 oz) barding fat (p. 21)

Serves 6–8
*Weighed without skin or bone

Peel and coarsely chop the onion, shallot, garlic and carrot. Roughly chop the leg of pork and veal and put, with the chopped vegetables, into a bowl with the parsley, oil, spice, nutmeg and generous seasonings of salt and pepper. Add the wine and leave in a cool place for 24 hours, turning everything over in the bowl from time to time. About 2 hours before cooking, add the truffle peelings and their juice (if used) to the sausage meat and mix thoroughly. Line a 1¼ litre (2 pint) capacity terrine with thin strips of barding fat and put in alternate layers of chopped meat and sausage meat. Strain the marinade, discard the vegetables and pour the liquid into the terrine. Cover with thin strips of barding fat and seal with foil and a lid on top. Put the terrine into a baking tin half filled with hot water and cook in the centre of a moderate oven preheated to 170°C, 325°F or Gas Mark 3 for 2 hours. Serve cold.

Terrine de Foie de Porc
Pig's Liver Terrine

300 g (12 oz) pig's liver
550 g (1¼ lb) fresh belly pork*
4 tablespoons brandy
15 g (½ oz) can truffle peelings
    (optional)
salt and ground black pepper
3 eggs
150 g (6 oz) barding fat (p. 21)

Serves 4–6
*Weighed without skin or bone

Mince the liver and pork and put into a basin with the brandy, truffle peelings and their juice (if used). Add salt and pepper to taste. Separate the eggs and stir the yolks into the mince. Whisk the whites until quite firm and then fold evenly into the mince. Line a 1 litre (1½–2 pint) capacity terrine with thin strips of barding fat, put in the mince, and cover with more strips of barding fat. Cover with kitchen foil and place the lid on top (or use two layers of foil if the dish has no lid). Stand in a baking tin with hot water to reach half way up the dish. Cook in the centre of a moderate oven preheated to 170°C, 325°F or Gas Mark 3 for about 1½ hours. The pâté is cooked when it has shrunk slightly from the sides of the terrine and the fat and juices are clear. Set aside until cold.

Pâté de Dinde
Turkey Pâté

1 medium onion
25 g (1 oz) butter
300 g (12 oz) cooked turkey meat
200 g (8 oz) fresh belly pork *or* pork
    and veal mixed
100 g (4 oz) crustless bread
a little milk
2 tablespoons coating Béchamel
    Sauce (p. 33)
1 egg, beaten
1 egg yolk
pinch mixed spice
½ teaspoon Worcestershire sauce
salt and ground black pepper

Serves 4–6

Peel and chop the onion and fry very gently in the butter until almost translucent. Mince the turkey and pork. Soak the bread in a little milk then squeeze out excess milk. Mix all these together thoroughly with the Béchamel Sauce, egg, egg yolk, spice, Worcestershire sauce and generous seasonings of salt and pepper. Pack into a buttered 750 ml (1½ pint) capacity terrine and cover with buttered kitchen foil. Set in a baking tin half filled with hot water and cook in a moderate oven preheated to 170°C, 325°F or Gas Mark 3 for about 1¼ hours. Serve cold.

Les Entremets et les Glaces

Puddings and Ices

On week days most French families finish their main meal with cheese and fresh fruit. The cheese always precedes the dessert, as a fitting partner to finish the wine served with the main course. But on Sundays and *fête* days an *entremet* is served as a treat.

Popular desserts such as fruit flans, *savarins*, *choux* pastries and *gâteaux* are generally bought from a local *pâtissier*, but many other simple desserts and carefully made *compôtes* of fruit, are prepared at home. Also included is a practical recipe for using stale croissants.

Les Crêpes Caramélisées
Glazed Pancakes

Make the pancake batter. Wash and dry the lemon or orange and finely grate the rind. Add to the batter with the rum or brandy before setting the batter to rest. Make the pancakes in the usual way (p. 29), then roll them up and arrange side by side on a flameproof serving dish. Keep hot in a warm oven until all are ready. Sprinkle the pancakes *evenly* with the caster sugar and put under a moderately hot grill until the sugar first melts and then caramelizes a little. Heat 1–2 tablespoons of rum or brandy, light, and pour flaming over the pancakes. Serve immediately, with a wedge of lemon for each portion.

Pancake Batter (p. 29)
1 lemon *or* orange
4 tablespoons rum *or* brandy
100 g (4 oz) caster sugar
rum or brandy for flaming
wedges of lemon for serving

Serves 8

Royale aux Noix
Nut Royal

Finely mince or grind the almonds and walnuts. Warm a mixing bowl, and in it cream the butter and sugar together until light and fluffy. Stir in the egg yolk and then the nuts. Whisk the egg white stiffly, then fold into the mixture. Line a rectangular tin of approximately 10 × 16 cm (4 × 6½ inches) with either greaseproof paper or kitchen foil. Mix the Kirsch and water together, dip each biscuit in it for a few seconds (no longer) and then arrange side by side in a single layer on the base of the tin. (If necessary trim the biscuits to fit the tin.) Cover with a layer of the nut mixture, then a layer of biscuits and so on alternately, finishing with biscuits. Cover the mould and refrigerate overnight. Shortly before serving unmould on to a serving dish and remove the lining paper. Decorate with whipped cream and halved walnuts.

25 g (1 oz) shelled and blanched
  almonds
25 g (1 oz) shelled walnuts
100 g (4 oz) butter
100 g (4 oz) caster sugar
1 large egg, separated
2 tablespoons Kirsch
1 tablespoon water
about 24 sponge finger biscuits
To decorate:
whipped cream
a few walnut halves

Serves 6–8

Vacherin aux Fraises
Strawberry Vacherin

The *vacherin* is based on flat circles of meringue which in France can be ordered from the local *pâtisserie*. To make it at home, proceed as follows. Cover two flat baking sheets with greaseproof paper or kitchen foil and mark a 20 cm (8 inch) diameter circle on each; brush lightly with oil. Put the egg whites into a large, clean, dry bowl and whisk steadily until firm, dry, and stiff enough to stand in peaks. Sprinkle in one-third of the vanilla-flavoured sugar and whisk until the meringue is again firm and standing in peaks. Repeat with another one-third of the sugar. Lightly fold in the remaining sugar with a tablespoon. Transfer the meringue to a piping bag fitted with a plain 1¼ cm (½-inch) tube. Starting in the centre, pipe a

Meringue
4 egg whites
200 g (8 oz) vanilla-flavoured caster
  sugar (p. 24)

Filling
450 g (1 lb) strawberries
1 teaspoon lemon juice
caster sugar
1 egg white
250 ml (½ pint) double cream

Serves 6–8

continuous flat spiral until the marked circles on the baking sheets are filled. Sprinkle with caster sugar and bake in the centre of a very cool oven 110°C, 225°F or Gas Mark ¼ for about 1½ hours, until dried out and crisp. Gently peel off the paper and cool on a wire rack.

Hull the strawberries and slice the large ones. Set aside some evenly shaped ones for decoration. Sprinkle with the lemon juice and sugar to taste. Whisk the egg white until stiff. Whisk the cream until thick and able to hold its shape; then fold the egg white into it. Sandwich the two meringue circles together with two-thirds of the cream and strawberries. Pile the remaining cream on top and decorate with the remaining strawberries.

Mousse aux Fruits Confits
Crystallized Fruit Mousse

100 g (4 oz) crystallized fruits
2 tablespoons Cointreau
300 g (12 oz) curd cheese
125 ml (¼ pint) single cream
vanilla-flavoured caster sugar (p. 24)
a little milk
sponge finger biscuits for serving

Serves 4

Chop the crystallised fruits into very small pieces, put into a bowl, add the Cointreau, stir well and leave for as long as possible.

Put the curd cheese into a bowl and mash it thoroughly with a fork. Stir in the cream, add sugar to taste and beat again thoroughly. Stir in the fruit and Cointreau. The mixture should be of whipped cream consistency but if too thick, beat in some cold milk very little at a time. Chill in the refrigerator. Pile into individual dishes and serve with sponge finger biscuits.

Pudding Duchesse
Duchess Pudding

250 ml (¼ pint) milk
65 g (2½ oz) vanilla-flavoured caster sugar (p. 24)
125 g (5 oz) dry macaroons
2 tablespoons Cointreau
50 g (2 oz) plain flour
50 g (2 oz) butter
2 egg yolks
3 egg whites
single cream for serving

Serves 4 or 5

Boil the milk with the sugar, then set aside to get cold. Place the macaroons between sheets of greaseproof paper and crush to fine crumbs with a rolling pin, then put into a bowl and stir in the Cointreau. Put the flour into a saucepan and, using a wire whisk, beat in the cold milk little by little. When perfectly smooth, set over low heat and stir continuously for 10 minutes. Take the pan off the heat, stir in the butter, beat well, and then add the egg yolks one at a time, beating for 2–3 minutes after each addition. Add the macaroon and Cointreau mixture and again beat thoroughly. Whisk the egg whites until firm then fold into the mixture lightly with an upward movement. Rinse an 18 cm (7 inch) diameter Charlotte mould or soufflé dish in cold water, drain but do not dry it. Pour in the mixture, and set the mould in a baking tin filled with warm water to reach half way up the mould. Cook in the centre of a preheated moderate oven 180°C, 350°F or Gas Mark 4 for 45–60 minutes, until firm to the touch. Leave the pudding to get cold before unmoulding it, and serve surrounded with cream.

Melon Fontainebleau
Fontainebleau Melon

Cut the cap off the stalk end of the melon and scoop out and discard the seeds. With a teaspoon, scoop out all the flesh in curls about the size of a walnut (or use a potato ball scoop) and put them in a basin with the Cointreau or Kirsch and a little sugar. Leave for at least 1 hour, then drain and reserve the juice. Beat the cream cheese and cream until smooth and light, add sugar to taste, and then fold in the melon curls and as much of the juice as you wish. Put this mixture into the melon shell, replace the cap, and refrigerate until ready to serve.

1 medium size ripe Cavaillon *or* Canteloup melon
2–3 tablespoons Cointreau *or* Kirsch
caster sugar
200 g (8 oz) French cream cheese, e.g. Petit Suisse
1–2 tablespoons double cream

Serves 6

Negresse à Plateau
Chestnut and Almond Dessert

This is a very rich sweet to be served in small portions. Chop the almonds, spread thinly on a small baking tray and toast lightly under the grill until golden, turning them frequently to prevent scorching. Cream the butter in a mixing basin, then beat in the chestnut purée thoroughly with a wooden spoon. Add the liqueur and three-quarters of the toasted nuts; beat well. Pile on to a serving dish, or into tiny individual dishes, and set aside to become very cold, refrigerating if possible. Just before serving, sprinkle with the remaining almonds.

50 g (2 oz) blanched almonds
65 g (2½ oz) butter
200 g (8 oz) can crème de marrons*
2 teaspoons Noyau liqueur

Serves 4
*A sweetened chestnut purée sold as chestnut spread

Gâteau Paresseux
Lazy Cake

Break the croissants into pieces in a basin. Bring the milk to the boil and pour over the croissants; leave for 15–20 minutes, then beat thoroughly with a whisk for 2 minutes, until fairly smooth. Set aside a few of the best walnut halves for decorating. Crush the rest and add them to the croissant mixture with all but 2 level tablespoons of the sugar. Stir the egg yolks one at a time into the mixture, followed by the cocoa and Cointreau. Whisk the egg whites until stiff and fold them lightly into the mixture. Butter a 1½ litre (2½ pint) capacity soufflé dish or casserole, pour in the mixture, decorate with the reserved walnuts and sprinkle with the remaining sugar. Bake in the centre of a preheated moderate oven 180°C, 350°F or Gas Mark 4 for 35–45 minutes depending on the depth of the mixture. Serve hot or cold, with lightly whipped cream scented with a little Cointreau, or with a fairly thin dark chocolate sauce.

4 stale croissants
500 ml (1 pint) milk
75 g (3 oz) shelled walnuts
150 g (6 oz) vanilla-flavoured caster sugar (p. 24)
2 eggs, separated
2 level tablespoons cocoa
1 tablespoon Cointreau
butter for greasing baking dish
whipped cream *or* thin chocolate sauce

Serves 6

Figues Chantilly
Figs with Cream

8 large fully ripe green figs
2 tablespoons Maraschino
125 ml (¼ pint) double cream
vanilla-flavoured caster sugar (p. 24)

Serves 4

Wipe the figs, and with a sharp, stainless knife cut them down from the stalk end into quarters, but without completely detaching them at the base. If necessary, open them out before sprinkling with 1 tablespoon of the liqueur. Whisk the cream with sugar to taste, and when stiff beat in the remaining liqueur. Pipe or spoon the cream into the centre of the figs.

Délices à la Crème
Cream Delights

12 sponge fingers*
200 g (8 oz) can sweetened chestnut
    purée
2 tablespoons Kirsch
250 ml (½ pint) whipping cream
1 level tablespoon caster sugar
6 half walnuts

Serves 6
*Sponge cake variety, not the
    biscuits

On the flat side of six sponge fingers spread a thick layer of the chestnut purée, then press the other sponge fingers on to the purée. Arrange the fingers side by side on a serving dish and sprinkle them with 1 tablespoon of the Kirsch. Whisk the cream until slightly thickened, then fold in the sugar and remaining Kirsch. Pour this over the fingers and garnish with the walnuts.

Soupe aux Cerises à la Française
French Cherry Soup

1 kg (2 lb) cherries*
500 ml (1 pint) hot water
rind of ½ lemon
    1 cm (⅓ inch) stick cinnamon
⅓ bottle red wine
2 level tablespoons potato flour
2 tablespoons cold water
caster sugar to taste
sponge finger biscuits

Serves 6–8
*Red Morello cherries or similar
    cooking variety

Stalk and stone the cherries, then set aside about 100 g (4 oz) of the best. Put the others into a saucepan with the water, the very thinly pared lemon rind and the cinnamon stick. Boil quickly for 8 minutes. Crush half of the stones and put into a basin. Bring the wine to the boil, pour over the stones and leave to infuse. Press the cooked cherries through a fine sieve with their liquid (or purée in an electric blender), and return to the pan. Mix the potato flour to a smooth cream with the water, stir into the cherry purée, add the whole cherries and sugar to taste. Bring to the boil, stirring continuously, then simmer for 4 minutes. Pass the wine through a strainer into the soup, let it heat through, then pour the soup into a tureen. At the last minute add some broken sponge finger biscuits.

Compôte d'Abricots
Poached Fresh Apricots

700 g (1½ lb) fresh apricots
250 ml (½ pint) water
150 g (6 oz) sugar
1 teaspoon lemon juice
1 tablespoon Kirsch *or* Cointreau
a few flaked almonds

Serves 4 or 5

Wash the apricots. Heat the water and sugar in a wide saucepan until the sugar has dissolved, then boil for 1–2 minutes. Add the apricots and poach very *gently* for 10–12 minutes, until tender, turning once. Remove the apricots with a perforated spoon to a shallow serving dish. Boil the syrup rapidly, uncovered, until reduced and syrupy. Take off the heat, stir in the lemon juice and liqueur, and pour over the fruit. Serve cold, with flaked almonds scattered over the top.

Pyramide de Pommes
Apple Pyramid

In a wide saucepan heat the water, sugar, lemon juice and cinnamon until the sugar has dissolved. Boil gently for 5 minutes. Meanwhile, peel and core the apples, and as prepared drop them immediately into the saucepan, turning them in the syrup to prevent browning. Poach very gently for 10–15 minutes until the apples are just tender, turning them once. It is important that the apples remain whole and do not break up. Remove from the syrup with a perforated spoon and arrange as a pyramid on a flameproof dish. Keep warm. Boil the syrup rapidly, uncovered, until reduced to about 125 ml (¼-pint), stir in the apricot jam and butter, and when hot pour over the apples.

To flame the dish, heat the rum, pour over the apples and ignite.

375 ml (¾ pint) water
100 g (4 oz) sugar
1 tablespoon lemon juice
2½ cm (1 inch) cinnamon stick
8 medium sized dessert apples
2 tablespoons apricot jam, sieved
25 g (1 oz) butter
4 tablespoons golden rum for flaming (optional)

Serves 4

Gâteau aux Cerises
Cherry Gâteau

Preheat a moderate oven 180°C, 350°F or Gas Mark 4. Put the sugar into a mixing bowl and leave in the oven to warm. Line a 20 cm (8 inch) diameter *moule à manqué* or deep sandwich tin with greaseproof paper, then brush the sides and bottom with oil and dust with flour. Whisk the sugar and eggs together steadily until the mixture is pale in colour and thick enough to leave a raised trail on the surface. Sift the flour and baking powder together twice, then fold lightly into the mixture. Turn into the prepared tin and bake in the centre of the oven until well risen and firm to touch. Partially cool in the tin, then turn out on to a wire rack.

Meanwhile beat the cheese with 2 tablespoons of the Kirsch and sugar to taste, until light and fluffy. Cut the cold sponge in half horizontally, sandwich with half of the filling and then spread top and sides with the remainder.

Strain the juice from the cherries into a small saucepan, add 1 level tablespoon sugar and heat gently until much reduced and thickened; stir in the rest of the Kirsch.

Just before serving arrange the cherries on top of the gâteau and pour the syrup over.

Sponge
75 g (3 oz) caster sugar
3 eggs
75 g (3 oz) plain flour
¼ teaspoon baking powder

Filling and topping
450 g (1 lb) curd cheese
3 tablespoons Kirsch
caster sugar
450 g (1 lb) can pitted Morello cherries

Serves 8

Croûtes aux Pêches
Peach Croûtes

8 small slices firm bread, about 1 cm
  (⅜ inch) thick
butter for spreading
4 large ripe peaches
a little caster sugar
3 heaped tablespoons redcurrant jelly
2 tablespoons water

Serves 4

Cut the bread into 7 cm (2½ inch) diameter circles. Spread generously with butter on both sides then place flat on the bottom of a shallow ovenproof dish. Skin the peaches (if necessary cover with boiling water for a few seconds to loosen the skin) then cut in halves and remove the stones. Roll the peaches in caster sugar, and place one half, rounded side up, on each of the bread croûtes. Cook in a preheated moderate oven 170°C, 325°F or Gas Mark 3 for 30 minutes.

Shortly before serving, put the redcurrant jelly and water into a small saucepan and heat gently, stirring, until smooth.

Serve hot, in the baking dish, with a little of the sauce over each.

Mousses Glacées au Liqueur
Iced Liqueur Mousses

2 large egg whites
250 ml (½ pint) double cream
100 g (4 oz) icing sugar,
  approximately
about 4 tablespoons Curaçao, Grand
  Marnier *or* brandy
50 g (2 oz) flaked toasted almonds

Serves 8

Set the refrigerator to its coldest setting.

Whisk the egg whites until stiff. In another basin, whisk the cream until beginning to thicken, then add the icing sugar and liqueur and continue whisking until thick and standing in peaks. Lightly but thoroughly fold in the egg whites. Spoon the mixture into individual containers (paper cases or cocotte dishes that will withstand freezing), and sprinkle with the nuts. Freeze until firm. When frozen, turn the refrigerator back to its normal setting.

Sorbet au Rhum
Rum and Lemon Sorbet

100 g (4 oz) granualted sugar
250 ml (½ pint) water
1 large lemon, well washed
1 orange
1 large egg white
1 tablespoon golden rum

Serves 4

Turn the refrigerator to its coldest setting.

In a small saucepan, heat the sugar in the water until dissolved, and then simmer steadily for exactly 10 minutes. Remove from the heat and immediately add the thinly pared rind of the lemon. Leave to infuse until absolutely cold. Add the squeezed orange and lemon juices, then strain the mixture into a chilled ice tray. Cover, and freeze until thick and mushy.

Whisk the egg white until stiff. Turn the semi-frozen ice into a basin, add the rum, and whisk to mix thoroughly. Fold in the egg white, return to the ice tray and continue freezing until firm.

Return the refrigerator to its normal setting.

About 30 minutes before serving, transfer the sorbet to the main part of the refrigerator to allow it to soften a little.

Glace aux Fruits
Fruit Ice Cream

Turn the refrigerator to its coldest setting.

Purée the fruit in an electric blender or by rubbing through a nylon sieve. (If using raspberries and an electric blender, first remove the pips by passing the purée through a nylon strainer.) Stir the lemon juice into the purée, with enough sugar to sweeten it rather well. Whisk the cream until slightly thickened but not stiff, then fold lightly but thoroughly into the purée.

Pour into shallow ice trays, cover, and freeze until firm. There is no need to beat this ice during freezing. When frozen, turn the refrigerator back to its normal setting. Half an hour or so before serving, transfer to the main part of the refrigerator to allow the ice to soften a little.

450 g (1 lb) raspberries *or* strawberries fresh *or* frozen
juice of ½ lemon
125–150 g (5–6 oz) icing sugar
250 ml (½ pint) double cream

Serves 6–8

Glace à la Vanille avec Variations
Vanilla Ice Cream

Turn the refrigerator to its coldest setting.

Put the egg yolks and sugar into a basin and beat with a wooden spoon until pale and creamy. Heat the milk and cream almost to boiling point, then stir gradually into the egg mixture. Strain into the top of a double boiler and cook over near boiling water, stirring constantly, until the custard thickens enough to coat the back of the spoon. (With care this can be done over direct heat, but watch it does not boil and curdle.) Remove from the heat and leave to cool, stirring from time to time. When cold, pour into a chilled ice tray, cover, and freeze in the freezing compartment until firm around the edges, about 30–45 minutes. Turn the ice into a basin, whisk vigorously, then return the tray and continue freezing until firm.

Turn the refrigerator back to its normal setting and allow the ice to ripen and mellow. Half an hour or so before serving, transfer to the main part of the refrigerator in order to allow the ice to soften a little.

3 large egg yolks
100 g (4 oz) vanilla-flavoured caster sugar (p. 24)
125 ml (¼ pint) milk
250 ml (½ pint) single cream

Serves 4

Glace au Kirsch
Add 2 tablespoons Kirsch to the *cold* custard just before freezing.

Glace au Citron
Add the finely grated rind of one scrubbed lemon to the cream and milk before heating. Stir 1 tablespoon lemon juice into the *cold* custard just before freezing.

Glace Plombière
Soak 50 g (2 oz) finely chopped glacé fruits in 2 tablespoons Cointreau for 1 hour or so. Fold into the vanilla ice when it is semi-frozen.

Index

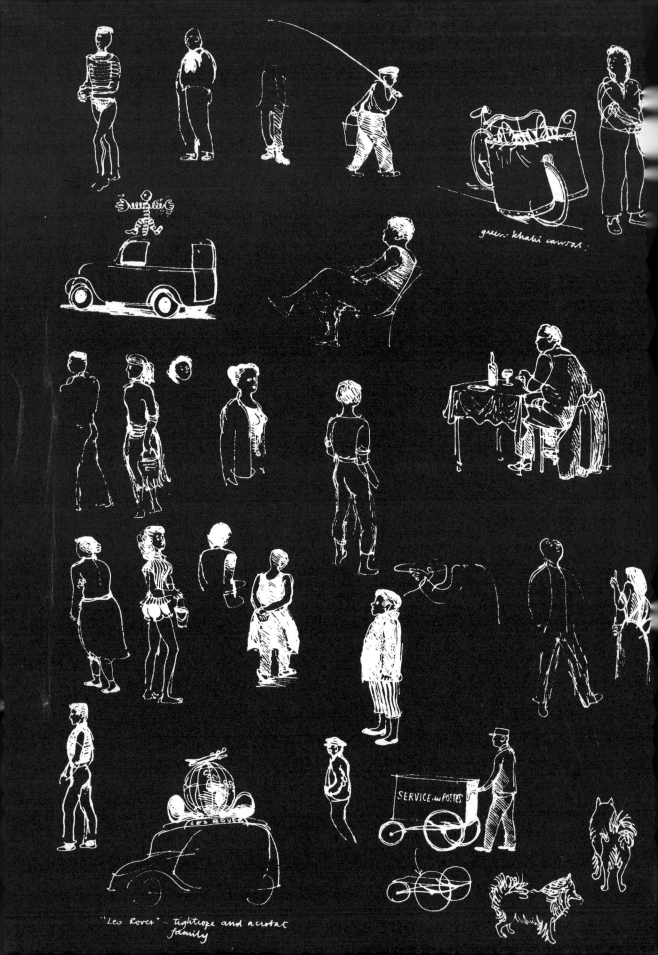

green-khaki canvas.

SERVICE des POSTES

"Les Rover" - tightrope and acrobat
family